15p

PICCOLO BOOK OF PARTIES
AND PARTY GAMES

By the same authors in Piccolo

PICCOLO BOOK OF GAMES FOR JOURNEYS

PICCOLO
BOOK OF PARTIES
AND PARTY GAMES

DEBORAH MANLEY AND PETA RÉE

Cover and text illustrations by David McKee

A Piccolo Original

PAN BOOKS LIMITED
LONDON

First published 1973 by Pan Books Ltd,
33 Tothill Street, London SW1

ISBN 0 330 23738 1

Printed in Great Britain by
Cox & Wyman Ltd,
London, Reading and Fakenham

CONTENTS

ACKNOWLEDGEMENTS

Acknowledgement is made to the following for permission to reprint their copyrighted material: Jonathan Cape Ltd for an extract from *The Oxus in Summer* by Katharine Hull and Pamela Whitlock, William Collins Sons & Co Ltd for an extract from *Little Grey Rabbit's Party* by Alison Uttley, John Farquharson Ltd for an extract from *The Railway Children* by E. Nesbit, George G. Harrap & Co Ltd for an extract from *Ameliaranne and the Green Umbrella* by Constance Heward, William Heinemann Ltd for an extract from *Then There Were Five* by Elizabeth Enright, David Higham Associates Ltd for extracts from *Christmas with the Savages* by Mary Clive and *The Wanderings of Mumfie* by Katherine Tozer, Mr C. R. Milne and Methuen & Co Ltd for an extract from *Winnie the Pooh* by A. A. Milne, and Mrs George Bambridge and Macmillan & Co Ltd for an extract from *Kim* by Rudyard Kipling.

HOW IT ALL STARTED

'It's my birthday soon,' said Harriet, 'can I have a party?'

'Well, I suppose so,' said Mother.

'Can we come?' asked Mark and Catherine and Adam, anxiously.

'Well, I suppose so,' said Harriet, 'but you mustn't be rude to my friends!'

'What shall we do at the party?' asked Adam.

'Eat lots of food,' said Mark, hopefully, patting his stomach.

'Play lots of games,' said Catherine, jumping up and down.

'Games where you can win prizes,' said Adam firmly.

'But not all that sort of game, because I never win anything,' said Catherine, even more firmly.

'It's my *party*, don't forget,' said Harriet, 'and I'll *decide who to invite*.'

'Well, I think we'd better sit down and make some plans,' said Mother.

And so they did.

PART ONE
Preparations

'If you please, Wise Owl,' said Grey Rabbit politely, 'we, that is, Squirrel, Hare and I, want to give a party, and we don't know how, and we thought you could tell us.'

'It's a long time since I was at a party,' said Wise Owl musingly. 'I forget whether it was a Christmas party, a birthday party, a tea party, or a Conservative party. But have you brought your present?'

Little Grey Rabbit held up the pot of jelly, and Owl, with a 'Humph!' of approval, ate it all up.

'Yes, not so bad,' said he. 'You must invite me to your party,' and he went back into the tree. Little Grey Rabbit sat waiting and wondering if he had finished, when the door of the beech-tree opened, and Wise Owl tossed a little red book from his library. How to Give a Party, it was called.

Little Grey Rabbit's Party *by Alison Uttley*

When you are going to give a party, the first thing to decide is how many people you are going to invite. This will probably be a compromise between the number you would actually like, and the number your mother thinks can possibly be fitted into your house or flat or garden. You might like to consider the idea of getting together with one or two other families and sharing a really big party, perhaps up to sixty children (any more than this is really no longer very pleasant). To do this you would probably have to hire a hall, which is quite possible, and not outrageously expensive, probably between £3 and £5. There would need to be at least six grown-ups to help with a party of this size.

Whatever size party you are giving, it is very important that there should be more than one grown-up there. A friend of ours was helping at a party at which one of the children, rushing to the door to greet her friends, fell and hit her head, and had to be taken to hospital by her mother. Our poor friend was left to cope with the party – but what would have happened if she had *not* been there? Fathers often tend to leave for the day when there's a children's party, but if you can persuade them to stay they usually make the party much more fun.

A good party doesn't just happen – it needs to be *planned*. The planning and preparations can be part of the fun for the party-givers, who may be making decorations and food and arranging things for several days in advance.

You may decide to give a party with a special theme, like a Hallowe'en party, a cowboys and Indians party or a fancy dress party. Invitations, decorations and food may all be designed to fit in with the theme.

Having decided on your guests and what sort of party you are giving, you should plan the programme – that is to say, what games you want to play and what order you want to play them in. It's a good idea to make a list, including all the things you need for each game, such as papers and pencils or blindfolds. It's best to start with games which people can join in as they arrive, and which will help them to get to know one another if they don't already.

You don't want all the games to be very active and noisy – especially after tea, it's a good idea to have some fairly gentle ones. It's better if quite a lot of games don't involve any one person winning, because then other people have, of course, to lose. If you are having prizes, you could give each person a bag with his or her name on it, to be kept in a special place, so that nothing gets lost.

4

If you can, make the party end in some style, rather than have it dwindle away as the guests depart. You may like to give your friends a small present when they go home. It can be fun to do this in some special way – in a lucky dip or treasure hunt, or with Father Christmas coming in with his sack.

Decorations

Mother fitted the forget-me-not crown on Bobbie's brown head.

'And now look at the table,' she said.

There was a cake on the table covered with white sugar, with 'Dear Bobbie' on it in pink sweets, and there were buns and jam; but the nicest thing was that the big table was almost covered with flowers – wallflowers were laid all round the tea-tray – there was a ring of forget-me-nots round each plate. The cake had a wreath of white lilac round it, and in the middle was something that looked like a pattern all done with single blooms of lilac or wallflower or laburnum.

'What is it?' asked Roberta.

'It's a map – a map of the railway!' cried Peter. 'Look – those lilac lines are the metals – and there's the station done in brown wallflowers. The laburnum is the train, and there are the signalboxes, and the road up to here – and those fat red daisies are us three waving to the old gentleman – that's him, the pansy in the laburnum train.'

'And there's Three Chimneys done in the purple primroses,' said Phyllis.

'And that little tiny rose-bud is Mother looking for us when we're late for tea. Peter invented it all, and we got all the flowers from the station.'

The Railway Children *by* E. Nesbit

The simplest way to make a room look ready for a party is to hang up a lot of balloons. You might like to welcome your guests even before they get into the house with a sign on the door. It might be a gaily coloured card saying:

> # WELCOME
> # TO
> # CATHERINE'S PARTY

with, perhaps a couple of balloons attached, or it might set the stage for the party theme.

We hope that the brief suggestions below will inspire you with some ideas of your own.

A Christmas Party

The door
A holly wreath with a big red bow.

The room
Paper chains, holly and mistletoe, tinsel and glitter, and of course THE TREE.

The table
A red cloth, or red and green napkins on a white cloth. Crackers.

Place cards made from laurel or holly leaves, with the names painted on in white paint.
A bowl of fruit mixed with evergreen leaves, nuts, and Christmas tree baubles.
A small Christmas tree.
A cake with snowy icing, decorated with robins or a Santa Claus on his sledge.
Red and green jellies.

A Spring Party

The door
A huge paper flower: a daffodil, perhaps.

The room
Yellow and green balloons.
Lambs, chicks, Easter bunnies, cut out from card, dangling from strings across the room.
Bowls of daffodils and other spring flowers.

The table
A yellow or white cloth with green napkins.
Decorated hard-boiled eggs as place cards, perhaps with funny faces on them.
A cake decorated with fluffy yellow chicks.
Green and yellow jellies or Bunny puddings (see page 34).

A May Party

The door
An enormous green paper leaf on the door, with 'welcome' written on it.

The room
Streamers from the centre of the ceiling to the walls, giving a Maypole effect.

The table
A white cloth with pink or blue napkins, decorated with flowers like Roberta's table in *The Railway Children*.
A paper flower at each place with a name tag attached.
A cake decorated with sugar flowers and encircled with green leaves.

An Autumn Party

The door
A big cut-out of a rosy apple.

The room
Press and dry a lot of autumn tinted leaves (see page 22) and fasten them to the walls with Blutack, so they won't leave any marks. Orange, green and brown paper chains.

The table
Brown, orange or white tablecloth with yellow napkins.
Dried autumn leaves with names written in white paint as place cards.
A pyramid of russet apples and oranges on a dish as a centre piece.
A chocolate cake.
Orange and red jellies.

A Hallowe'en Party

Ask everyone to come dressed as a witch or warlock, with a black mask.

A Jack-o'-Lantern made from a hollowed-out pumpkin or large swede, with a candle inside, glowing at the window.

The room
Black and orange paper chains.
Cut-outs of cats, witches and skeletons on the walls.

The table
An orange cloth with red napkins.
Black cats for place cards.
A big bowl of red apples.
Gingerbread men.
Orange and red jellies.

A Cowboy Party
The guests come dressed as cowboys, the host wears a sheriff's badge.

The door
A big sign saying:

HITCH YOUR HORSES HERE

The room
Signs on the walls saying such things as 'Use the spittoons',
'Park your firearms here' and 'Don't shoot the pianist'.
Horseshoes, lassos and cowboy hats hung on the walls.

The table
A checked cloth with red napkins.
Toy cowboys holding place names.
A horseshoe-shaped cake.

A Kings and Queens Party

The door
A scroll saying 'Welcome to the Palace'.

The room
Gold and silver paper chains, gold and silver Christmas
tree balls.

The table
A white cloth with gold and silver doilies fixed to it.
A golden crown for everyone to wear, with their place name
on it.
A white cake with a gold or silver cake frill and red candles.
Red jellies.

A Fun Fair Party

The door
Sign saying 'All the fun of the fair!'
Paper flags strung from the windows.

The room
Broad red and white crepe paper streamers strung from the
centre of the ceiling to the walls to look like a marquee.

Lots of balloons.

Stalls set up round the room, with games on them (see page 136).

The table

A bright coloured cloth with tinsel laid across it.

Clown place cards.

Carousel jellies (see page 33).

A cake iced red and white in divisions, and with red and white candles.

At a Red Indian Party you could give each guest an Indian head-dress as he arrives. These are made from feathers

and corrugated wrapping paper. If it is autumn and pheasants are in season, ask the butcher well in advance if he would keep some feathers for you. Cut strips of the corrugated paper big enough to fit around your forehead with a slight overlap. Cut *across* the lines of corrugation – this gives you holes to stick the feathers into. Staple the ends of the strip together to make a circle, and stick three or four feathers in the holes. The feathers are worn at the back of the head; you could draw some decorations on the front of the band with felt-tip pens.

You could also have a fairy party, where all the guests are given wings and wands as they come in, a football party, a railway party, an astronaut party, a circus party, and so on.

Invitations

The Fish-Footman began by producing from under his arm a great letter, nearly as large as himself, and this he handed over to the other, saying in a solemn tone, 'For the Duchess. An invitation from the Queen to play croquet.' The Frog-Footman repeated, in the same solemn tone, only changing the order of the words a little, 'From the Queen. An invitation for the Duchess to play croquet.' Then they both bowed, and their curls got entangled together.

Alice's Adventures in Wonderland *by Lewis Carroll*

You can invite your friends by word of mouth, or over the telephone, but somehow a party is more exciting to look forward to if you have been sent a written invitation. You can, of course, buy party invitation cards, but you might prefer to make your own. If you are giving a party with a theme, you can begin to set the scene with the invitation card.

It is best to invite your friends well in advance – about ten to fourteen days – so that they have time to reply.

The important things which must appear on the invitation card are: the day, the date, the time the party begins and the time it ends, the place where it is being held, a telephone number (if there is one), and, of course, your name. You could also provide a tear-off reply card. In any case, an invitation should always be replied to – otherwise the people giving the party won't know how many guests to expect.

Here are some ideas for making your own invitation cards; first a few for any party and then a few for special parties.

1 For this card you need some coloured card, letters and words cut from magazines, some glue and a felt-tip pen. Cut the card into pieces 4 inches by 12 inches and fold them in half. Open the card out and write your message with a combination of cut-out words and letters (from old magazines and newspapers) and your felt-tip pen across the inside of the card. Then fold it again and write in big letters A PARTY! across the front. The card might look like this, but of course everyone's will be slightly different. You may have to cut your card to a different size to fit your envelopes.

2 For this card you need a seed or bulb catalogue or gardening magazine, some coloured card, scissors, glue and a felt-tip pen.

Cut the card into pieces 4 inches by 12 inches. Fold each card in half to make a card 4 inches by 6 inches. Cut out a selection of flowers from the catalogues or magazines. Write the words of your invitation inside the front of the card and write a tear-off reply form on the inside of the back of the card. Decorate the front of the card by glueing flowers onto it. Put a few small flower pictures among the words on the inside of the card. Stick a flower onto each envelope when you are ready to send out the cards.

You could use other pictures of course – footballers, animals, cars, and so on.

Here is the sort of wording you might like to use for the invitation and reply:

I am having a party on January 24th
from 4 until 7 o'clock at
15 Brown Road. I hope you will
be able to come.

I can / cannot come to your party.
My name is...................................

3 Here is an idea for a long card which can be hung up. You need coloured card from an art shop, some coloured sticky backed paper, a felt-tip pen, a punch and some ribbon or string. Cut out pieces of card 4 inches wide and 18 inches long. Fold the card in thirds, so each piece is 4 inches wide and 6 inches long so that it will fit into an envelope. The invitation itself will be on the two top sections of the card; the space for the reply card will be on the bottom third. Draw an outline picture on the top pieces of the card, write your message inside the outline and decorate it with the sticky paper. Write the reply card on the bottom piece. Punch a hole in the top and put string through it so it can be hung up.

Invitations for special parties

If your party is going to have a special theme or be on a special occasion you can show this on the card.

A Fancy Dress Party

You need light-weight white card, felt-tip pens or paints, a

pencil and scissors. Cut cards 12 inches by four inches. Fold the card in four, first in half and then again in half so that you have a 'concertina' card 3 inches by 4 inches. Draw an outline figure on the front piece – a girl in a long dress or a boy in trousers with hands held out on both sides like this:

17

Cut round the outline without cutting where the hand is, so that when you open out the card you have four figures holding hands like this:

Write your invitation on the first figure. Write a tear-off reply card on the last figure. Colour the two middle figures in costumes of different kinds. Your finished card might look like one of these:

A Hallowe'en Party

Here are two ideas. For both
you need some orange card.
For the first one you also need
some black tissue paper, glue,
scissors and a felt-tip pen and
a pencil. Cut out cards 8
inches by 4 inches and fold
them to make cards four inches

square. The fold is at the top of the card. Draw the outline
of a pumpkin on the card like this, and cut round it, making

sure that the two pieces are still
joined at the fold. With a pair of
sharp scissors cut out holes for eyes,
nose and mouth from the top card
only like this: Cut out a piece of
black tissue paper large enough to
be stuck over the back of the jack-
o'-lantern face, so that the features show up black. Write
your invitation with the felt-tip pen on the inner sheet of
the card.

For the second sort of card you need the orange card,
some black paper, a piece of plain card, a pencil, scissors,
glue and a felt-tip pen. Cut out a card from the orange
card 4 inches by 12
inches and fold it in half,
with the fold down the
side. On the plain card
draw the outline of the
figure of a witch riding
a broomstick. Here is an
outline for you to draw
it from:

Cut out the figure on
the card and use it for a stencil or shape to draw around.

Draw round it onto the black paper. Cut out your black witches and stick them on to the front of the orange cards. Write your invitation inside with the felt-tip pen.

A Bonfire Party

Here is one idea for an invitation to a bonfire party. It might be a good idea to write out the recommendations for bonfire parties made by the Firework Makers' Guild (see page 26) and slip them in with your invitations.

You need some black card, some white paper, some yellow, orange and red tissue paper, a felt-tip pen, glue and a brown crayon. Cut cards 12 inches by 4 inches and fold to make cards 6 inches by 4 inches. Cut out 'flames' from the tissue paper of different sizes up to $2\frac{1}{2}$ inches long and of slightly different shapes, but basically as shown in the drawing.

Stick the flames onto the front of the card from a central point alternating the colours, but leaving the tips free. Draw the logs and sticks of the fire at the base of the flames with the brown crayon. Cut a piece of the white paper 5 inches by 3 inches. Write the words of your invitation on it and stick this sheet inside the card. You might decorate the envelope in the top left-hand corner with another bonfire drawn with felt-tip pens.

A Christmas Party

Here are two ideas for invitations at Christmas time. For the first one you need bits of red, yellow and green card, a felt-tip pen, a pencil and scissors. Cut the card into rectangles of about 12 inches by 4 inches and fold them to make cards 4 inches by 6 inches with the fold at the top. Now draw outlines on the cards, as big as will fit on to them – a Christmas tree on the green ones, a bell on the yellow ones and a Christmas tree decoration on the red ones. Part of the outline must overlap the fold at the top of the card, like this:

Now cut out round the outline on both sides of the card. Write your invitation on the inside of the front of the card and your reply card on the back, so that it can be torn off and sent back.

For the second card you need red card, white paper, some cotton wool, a black felt-tip pen, a pencil, scissors and glue. Cut out cards 6 inches by 4 inches. Draw the outline of Father Christmas on the card, like this:

Cut out this outline. Draw arms on the card, joined across the stomach. Cut out small pieces of white paper in the shape of hands and face and stick them onto the figure of Father Christmas like this:

Stick little pieces of cotton wool onto the chin. Draw a face above the beard. Now with a pair of sharp pointed scissors cut a slit just above Father Christmas's hands. On pieces of paper write your invitation. Fold these up and slip them into the slit so that it looks as if Father Christmas is holding the invitation.

An Autumn Party

Collect a number of autumn leaves which are not very big
– about three inches across – and have turned pretty colours.
Press and dry them by placing them between sheets of
paper and putting them into a heavy book. Always put
sheets of paper between your leaves and the pages of the
book or you may mark the book. Leave them for about a
week.

When you are ready to make the cards you will need some
coloured card, some strong glue such as Uhu, a felt-tip
pen and scissors. Cut out cards 12 inches by 4 inches and
fold them to make cards 6 inches by 4 inches. Fix a leaf
onto the front of each card. Write your invitation inside
with the felt-tip pen. If you want your guests to wear
special clothes for the theme of the party, remember to
say so on the invitation.

A Fairy Party

For a party with the theme of fairies you can make a very
pretty stand-up invitation card. You will need some pale
coloured card, some tissue paper, a pencil, some silver
glitter, some felt-tip pens and glue.

Cut out pieces of card 4 inches by 6 inches. Draw on
them a shape like this:

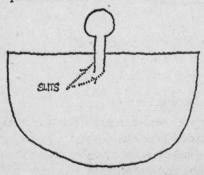

From the tissue paper cut out a pair of wings, like this:

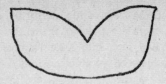

Cut slits in the neck as shown. Slip the wings into these

slits and glue them behind the head and neck. Now make a face for the fairy and decorate her with silver glitter. Write the invitation on her back and write along one edge of her skirt at the back 'I will stand up if you fix this edge to the other edge'. This is what the fairy will look like when the edges are fixed together.

A Cowboys and Indians Party

For this you will need one small feather for each guest, some card, scissors and a felt-tip pen. Cut out cards about 6 inches by 4 inches. Make a double slit across one corner as shown in the drawing on page 25.

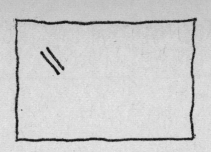

Fix the feather through the slit, then write your message of invitation on the remainder of the card.

COME TO A PARTY WITH THE OTHER COWBOYS AND INDIANS at................. on.................

25

Conflagrations

. . . My birthday falls on the fifth of November. From this it came about that I always had to bear a good many jokes about being burnt as a Guy Fawkes; but, on the other hand, I was allowed to make a small bonfire of my own, and to have eight potatoes to roast therein, and eight pennyworth of crackers to let off in the evening. A potato and a pennyworth of crackers for every year of my life.

Old Father Christmas *by Juliana Horatia Ewing*
First published 1888

If your birthday falls on or near November 5th, you might like to celebrate it with a Bonfire Party and fireworks. For this kind of party it is *essential* to have a responsible grown-up in charge.

You can have sparklers for each child to hold, but otherwise *all* fireworks should be let off by the responsible grown-up. Below is the Firework Code prepared by the Firework Makers' Guild, which you should study. Note especially Number 8; every year *thousands* of pets have to be put down by the RSPCA because they have been injured through fright at fireworks.

THE FIREWORK CODE

1. Keep fireworks in a closed box; take them out one at a time and put the lid back at once.

2. Follow the instructions on each firework carefully; read them by torchlight – never a naked flame.
3. Light fireworks at arm's length – preferably with a safety firework lighter or fuse wick.
4. Stand well back.
5. Never return to a firework once lit – it may go off in your face.
6. Never throw fireworks.
7. Never put fireworks in your pocket.
8. Keep pets indoors.
9. Never fool with fireworks.

It is difficult to believe that *anybody* could be silly enough to do most of these things; but apparently they are.

You can have a Guy, made of old clothes stuffed with rags and straw, to burn on the fire. Each child can be given a mask to wear. You will find suggestions for food on page 35, if you want to eat outside. Otherwise you go indoors and have a normal party spread.

Wiener Roast
You don't really have to wait till November 5th for an excuse to have a Bonfire Party. When we were children in Canada, our favourite sort of party was a Wiener Roast. Wieners are what in England are called frankfurters; in fact, you can use ordinary chipolata sausages if you prefer (they're cheaper, too!).

Most of the Wiener Roasts we went to were held on the beach nearby, which is obviously the safest and best place for such a party. The guests played games until dusk began to fall; then the fire was lit, and when it was burnt up enough each guest was given a strong green branch, about three to four feet long, with the end shaped to a point. On this the sausages were speared and held into the flames to cook.

Until you have tasted a half-charred frankfurter, hot and redolent with wood-smoke, clapped into a long, soft roll spread with tomato ketchup or French mustard, you don't begin to know what a 'hot dog' is really like. It bears very little resemblance to the anaemic boiled objects with limp onions served up by most hot dog stands. Hot dogs are naturally the most important food at a Wiener Roast (you should have three or four for each person), but marshmallows roasted on sticks are also traditional, and as well you can have the kind of food suggested for a Guy Fawkes party.

Usually there was a sing-song around the fire when everybody had eaten enough – all the old favourites, including round songs, such as the two suggested below. A round song is sung by the party being split up into four groups, then the first group begins with the first line, and as it goes onto the second line, the second group starts with the first line, and so on until everyone is singing. The sound starts fairly soft, builds up as more and more people are singing, and then dies away again, as each group finishes its verse.

Fire's Burning (to the tune of *London's Burning*)
Fire's burning, fire's burning,
Draw nearer, draw nearer,
In the gloaming, in the gloaming.
Come sing and be merry.

Row your Boat
Row, row, row your boat,
Gently down the stream,
Merrily, merrily, merrily, merrily.
Life is just a dream.

As with the Guy Fawkes party, there must be a grown-up

in charge of the fire; and you must be sure the fire is absolutely out before you leave.

So much for conflagrations – but it's worth mentioning here various other kinds of 'different' parties.

Older children may prefer the 'outing' type of party. If you live near a canal or river you can give a party on a canal boat as it cruises along. With smaller groups, probably not more than eight at the most, you could go to a film, the circus, a play, a museum or a special 'sight' such as the Tower of London. You then go home to a high tea.

A rather eccentric party is the Neighbourhood Meal. This is only possible if you live in a community in which a lot of children live close together, and their parents know each other well. Briefly, it means that the guests go from house to house, having one course of each meal at each one, perhaps with a game or two at each house.

Another sort of party very popular with girls in Canada was a Pyjama Party or Slumber Party. This consisted of half a dozen girls going to a friend's house for supper and staying for the night and for breakfast (which they cooked and washed up themselves – all part of the fun). Ghost-story telling, confidence swapping and a great deal of giggling went on far into the night.

Collations

... *never has there been such a feast before or since. Pantry boys, well scrubbed for the occasion, and in spotless white jackets, hurried here and there handing round trays of little cakes, the kind with white and pink and chocolate icing, with violets and silver bobbles on top – and marzipan for those who liked it. There were bowls of steaming punch made from fruit and ginger wine; jugs of ginger beer and great glasses of lemon and orange juice with straws to suck them up through: in fact there was anything you liked to ask for.*

Down the centre of the tables were arranged bowls of jelly beautifully decorated, and great trifles, all almonds, angelica and cream, and of course an enormous Christmas cake, layers and layers of white icing, with snow babies playing about on top. By each place was a bundle of fat crackers which rattled satisfactorily when you shook them to see what was inside.

The Wanderings of Mumfie *by Katherine Tozer*

It is not always easy to decide how much food you need for a party. Sometimes being in company seems to make people hungrier than usual – and sometimes not. You do want to have plenty, but you don't want to have too much left over; you don't want to be eating jelly for breakfast for days to come! Nor, if there is a birthday cake to be eaten at the end, do you want to make your guests so full that they can't bear to eat it. (Hasn't that happened to you before now?) One way of avoiding this misfortune is to have *all* the food on show when your guests start eating – don't have jellies and cakes hiding in the wings until everyone is too full to enjoy them. If all is revealed at the start, people can plan to their own capacity. But you could also have emergency stocks of crisps and biscuits and other things that will keep that you can bring out in case everything disappears.

On the whole it's better to have a sit-down meal than a stand-up one (less mess on the floor, for one thing), but if you have a very large number of people, you may have to have a serve-yourself, or buffet, meal. If you are giving the party in your garden, you could have the spread laid out on a trestle table for everyone to help themselves; this would also avoid having to carry out a lot of chairs. Besides, egg, jam and ice cream, well-trodden in, is less harmful to lawns than to carpets!

Here are a few suggestions for food, with some indications of the quantities you will need.

Sandwiches

Can be of bread, white and brown, or soft rolls. Many people prefer open sandwiches. If you have closed sandwiches it is a good idea to have little flags on the plates, saying what is inside, so that people don't help themselves to anything they don't like.

Allow one to one and half rounds of sandwiches or two rolls per head, depending on the age of your guests. It takes about half a pound of butter to cover thirty slices of bread. Thin sliced bread is easiest.

SOME FILLINGS

Cold scrambled, or chopped hard-boiled, egg, mixed with mayonnaise to hold it together.
Peanut butter and tomato ketchup or honey.
Sliced tomato, well salted and peppered.
Cream cheese and chopped walnuts.
Cheese and chutney.
Sardine mashed with a little lemon juice or vinegar.
Chocolate spread.
Mashed banana.
Hundreds and thousands (open sandwiches only).
Sandwiches can be made quite early on the day of the party and stored in the fridge wrapped in foil.

Savouries

Often more popular than sweet things.
Small chipolata sausages on cocktail sticks.
Small cubes of cheese and chunks of pineapple together on cocktail sticks.
Cheese straws.
Peanuts.
Potato crisps in varied flavours.
Dips; these are served in bowls, with plates of crisps or

cheesy biscuits to dip with. You could have a cheese and tomato dip, a mushroom dip, even an avocado dip for more sophisticated tastes.

Sweet food

Tiny meringues.
Minute cakes (about two bite-size) iced in as many bright colours as possible – red, blue, bright yellow, green, etc.
Chocolate krispies.
Shortbread.
Iced biscuits.
Trifle (about 12 trifle sponges, 1 lb tinned fruit, 1 pint jelly and 1 pint custard will serve 6 people).
Ice cream (a family block serves 5 to 6).
Jellies (1 pint serves 4 to 5). Jellies are nicer and more interesting if made with tinned or fresh fruit, using the juice from the tin for as much of the liquid as possible. For example, make orange jellies with mandarin oranges, raspberry or strawberry jellies with tinned or fresh fruit, and lemon jellies with small chunks of raw apple. All these can be served in small paper dishes, with whipped cream on top if you like.

CAROUSEL JELLIES

Twist thin strips of two contrasting coloured crepe papers round a wooden skewer or the handle of a wooden spoon. Stick it in a bowl of sand to make it stand upright, or perhaps an apple or orange if you use a skewer. Join as many ribbons of paper as you have guests to the top of this 'pole', and lead each twisted strip to a bowl of jelly, either standing the bowl on the end of the ribbon, or fastening it with sellotape.

BUNNY PUDDINGS

Decorate a glass with a stem with a bunny face, perhaps stick whiskers on it. You can do this with strips of sticky paper. Fill the glass with ice cream or mousse and stick two sponge fingers (sold as 'boudoir biscuits', we regret to say) to form the rabbit's ears.

It is somehow less overwhelming and more attractive to have lots of small plates and dishes of food rather than a few large platters.

THE BIRTHDAY CAKE

This may be made in a shape such as an engine, a fort, a car or doll's pram (use crystallized orange slices for the wheels), or decorated as a clock face, a chessboard, a flower garden, a maypole (a wooden skewer in the middle with thin ribbons to candle-holding figures at the edge). Small model cowboys, Indians, knights, animals, etc, can all be used as decorations. (The boy in our family once had a brilliant green iced cake with a footballer on it, to his great pleasure.)

Drinks

Fruit squash – should be made in advance, in big jugs. Add ice cubes at the last minute, and a slice of orange or lemon on the edge of the jug will make it look more attractive. One bottle makes 18 glasses.

Milk – plain or flavoured.

Tea.

Bonfire Party Food

Hot sausages.

Hot tomato soup served in mugs, poured from thermos flasks.

Hot baked potatoes in their jackets, split, buttered and salted, in tin foil for easy holding. If you want to cook them in the ashes of the fire, more than half-cook them at home first, as baked potatoes take *at least* an hour.

)-PBPG-C

Halved tomatoes and chunks of cucumber.
Gingerbread men.
Parkin.
Spicy biscuits.
If you have a cake it would need to be a fairly solid and non-messy one – no creamy or flaky icing.
Apples and bananas.
Cocoa and/or coffee.

PART TWO
The Games

Harriet invited twenty-three children to her party, twelve girls and eleven boys. Their names were Clare, Catherine, Miranda, Jane, Julie, Michelle, Pauline, Maria, Imogen, Jessica, Sophie, and Morag, and Philip, Tom, Peter, Mark, James, John, Darren, Adam, Michael, Leo and Gideon.

This book is dedicated to them all.

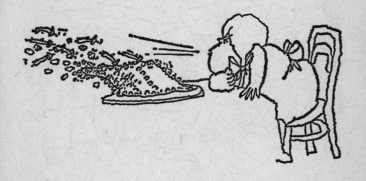

Organization

The guests have accepted, you've decided what sort of party you are giving, and what food and decorations you will have. The last important thing to plan is your programme of games. It is worth thinking fairly carefully about this for a lot of reasons.

One thing you must consider is the sort of guests you have invited – how old they are, what kind of skills they have – can they, for instance, *all* read? If only some of them can, it is not fair to have games in which reading is necessary; and the same of course goes for writing. Perhaps one of your friends is handicapped in some way. For example, it may not be possible to have all the games of a kind that a child who cannot run can take part in, but you would have to make sure that there were as few as possible, and that they were widely spaced out. Some active games, like General Post (page 53) need someone to call out things, and so your friend could do this, and not be left out.

Again, many people are very shy, particularly at the beginning of a party. For this reason you should start off with games in which one person doesn't have to be noticeable, but in which, on the other hand, nobody can just get left in a corner. If you have acting games, unless everyone knows each other very well, it may be better to do acting in teams.

Then there's the question of competitions and prizes. Young children often feel anxious and upset if they have to compete, although older children generally like it. It is perhaps better not to have prizes at a younger-age party. In any case, prizes should always be trifling, such as a felt-tip pen, a small chocolate bar, an animal-shaped rubber or a card of coloured sticky seals. An exception might be made for a Treasure Hunt, when the prize could be more imposing. We once made a small 'Treasure chest' of cardboard and filled it with golden chocolate coins, and wine gums for jewels.

As we said earlier, you should try to get a good mix of games, not all noisy and active, nor too many quiet ones one after another. Probably about two-thirds active to one-third quieter games is about right, with possibly nothing very wild for the first half-hour after tea. This is a counsel of perfection, for our experience is that, after sitting (fairly) quietly for 20–30 minutes over tea, the boys particularly tend to explode into action. If you are having a film show or conjuror, after tea is the time to have them; otherwise you will have to think of something fairly interesting if you want to stop your guests shaking their teas about inside them.

Write a list of the games in order, and a list of any 'props' you need – pencils, paper, balloons, balls, records, etc – and make sure that enough of each are gathered together in a safe place on the day. Start with a game which people can join in as they arrive without spoiling it. You could prevent any awkwardness about choosing sides for team games by allotting the guests alternately to a team as they arrive, pinning on a different coloured bit of ribbon for each team. You could follow your party theme in some way; a Wild West party gives you two natural teams!

Here is the kind of list you might make for a party of under-eights, which is to last about three hours:

Pass the Parcel (page 112)
Crusts and Crumbs (page 77)
General Post (page 53)
Pass the Orange (page 78)
Blow the Balloon (page 76)
Jumble Sale (page 113)
Musical Fancy Dress (page 114)

TEA (which will take less time than you hope, maybe only 20 minutes)

One more thing about the programme – be flexible. If a game is not going well, finish it quickly and get on to the next one; it's a good idea to have one or two extra ones up your sleeve. On the other hand, if a game is a roaring success, play it again if the guests want to; don't hurry on to the next game just because the list says so.

Mix and Match

The animals went in two by two,
Vive la compagnie!

At the beginning of a party, you want something going on to keep people occupied while they wait for all the guests to arrive or, if all the guests do not know each other, to mix them up and get them to meet each other. Sometimes you may also want games to make up pairs for other games.

Picture Match

Cut up a number of postcards or old Christmas cards into 2, 3 or 4 pieces. Mix them up in a box. Each guest takes one and then has to find the other people who have the pieces which belong with it to make up the complete picture.

This is a good game to play when you want to divide the guests up into groups for later games or into teams.

What Goes with What?

Write groups of words which match on separate pieces of paper. Your groups for a party of twelve which you wanted to divide into four groups of three might be:

    needle, pins, thread;
    drake, duck, duckling;
    butcher, baker, candlestick maker;
    apples, oranges and pears.

Mix up the pieces of paper. Give one to each person and ask them to find their partners.

You can use Happy Family cards for this game, with people looking for the Mr, Mrs, Miss and Master of their family.

Baby Show

Ask the guests to bring with them a photograph of themselves as babies. Put each picture in a small numbered plastic envelope or cellophane bag and pin them up around the room. Guests have to guess which baby has grown into which guest. They write down the number of the picture and the name of the guest they think it is.

This game needs to be played by people who know each other at least a bit.

Silhouettes

To prepare for this game you need a soft pencil or felt-tip pen, a pad of paper and a bright light. Fix the light so that it falls on to a sheet of paper which you pin on the wall.

As each guest arrives, get them to sit between the light and the paper so that their shadow falls on the paper. Quickly outline the shadow on the paper and pin up the next sheet for the next 'sitter'. When you have all the silhouettes ready, write a number on each one and pin them up round the room. The guests then go round and try to guess which numbered picture represents which guest. If you like, give a prize to the one with most correct guesses.

Who Am I?
Pin a label bearing the name of a famous real or fictional person on the back of each guest as they arrive. They then circulate and ask questions to find out who they are. You can make the game more difficult by allowing only Yes and No answers, or only allowing each person to ask one question of each other person at a time.

The game might go like this:

ADAM: Am I a man?

MICHELLE: No.

ADAM: Am I a real person?

PAULINE: Yes.

ADAM: Am I alive now?

LEO: No.

ADAM: Am I Queen Victoria?

HARRIET: No.

ADAM: Was I alive when Queen Victoria was alive?

JESSICA: Yes.

ADAM: Oh, am I Florence Nightingale?

MARK: Yes, you are.

This can be used as a 'pairing game' if the guests are given names which pair together. Examples are: Tom and Jerry, Laurel and Hardy, Robin Hood and Maid Marian, Red Riding Hood and Wolf, Jack and Jill, Albert and Victoria, Miss Muffet and Spider, Beauty and the Beast, Robinson Crusoe and Man Friday, Tweedledum and Tweedledee.

You might use instead the name of things that go together, such as: salt and pepper, bread and butter, strawberries and cream, oranges and lemons, sugar and spice, oil and vinegar.

For a party of older people, the names of books which have an 'and' in the title might be used: *Cakes and Ale*, *The Moon and Sixpence*, *Pride and Prejudice*, *Sense and Sensibility*, *Fathers and Sons*, *War and Peace*, *Dombey and Son*.

Alternatively, you might make pairs, one of whom wore a label with the name of a book, and the other with the name of its author.

What Am I?

As the guests arrive they are each given a piece of paper with the name of a rather obscure animal on it. By obscure, we mean difficult to draw as much as anything – like an anteater, a bush baby, a dinosaur, a rhinoceros, a rattlesnake or a flamingo. Each guest draws the animal on the other side of the piece of paper and then pins it on his chest, drawing side out. The guests then walk about, trying to guess each other's animals and have their own guessed. They write down their guesses and the one who guesses the most correctly in a given time is the winner.

Noah's Ark
Write the names of two each of a collection of rather noisy animals on pieces of paper and mix them up. Animals like ducks, dogs, owls, donkeys, cats would do. Each guest takes an animal name and then makes its noise until he or she finds a partner who is making the same noise; then they are ready to go into the Ark two by two.

If you are having some songs at the party you might like 'the animals' to try this one:

One More River
The animals came in two by two,
   Vive la compagnie.
The centipede with the kangaroo.
   Vive la compagnie!
     One more river, and that's the river of Jordan,
     One more river and that's the river to cross.

The animals came in three by three.
  Vive la compagnie.
The elephant on the back of the flea.
  Vive la compagnie!
    One more river, etc.

The animals came in four by four,
  Vive la compagnie.
The fat hippopotamus got stuck in the door.
  Vive la compagnie!
    One more river, etc.

The animals came in five by five,
  Vive la compagnie.
Some were dead and some were alive.
  Vive la compagnie!
    One more river, etc.

The animals came in six by six,
  Vive la compagnie.
The monkey, he was up to his tricks.
  Vive la compagnie!
    One more river, etc.

The animals came in seven by seven.
  Vive la compagnie.
Some went to Hell, and some went to Heaven.
  Vive la compagnie!
    One more river, etc.

The animals came in eight by eight,
  Vive la compagnie.
The worm was early, the bird was late.
  Vive la compagnie!
    One more river, etc.

The animals came in nine by nine,
   Vive la compagnie.
Some had water and some had wine.
   Vive la compagnie!
      One more river, etc.

The animals came in ten by ten,
   Vive la compagnie.
If you want any more you must sing it again.
   Vive la compagnie!
      One more river, and that's the river of Jordan,
      One more river and that's the river to cross.

Paul Jones
A quick way to select partners. The guests form two circles one inside the other. Music is played and the inner circle goes round clockwise, the other circle anti-clockwise. When the music stops, the person who you are facing in the other circle is your partner.

Sometimes you are not looking for ways to match people, but for ways to sort out one person from the others – to decide who should be 'he' in a game of tag, for instance. Then you can 'dib'. Here are some verses for dibbing.

   Inter, mitzy, titzy, tool.
   Ira, dira, dominu,
   Oker, poker, dominoker,
   Out goes you.

   Eeny, meeny, miney, mo,
   Catch a monkey by his toe;
   If he squeals, let him go,
   Eeny, meeny, miney, mo.

One potato, two potato,
Three potato, four,
Five potato, six potato,
Seven potato, more.

(For this dib, all the players hold their fists out in front
of them. One player counts out their fists one by one;
when he reaches 'more', that fist is withdrawn from the
circle. The dibbing goes on until only one 'potato' is left.)

Eetle ottle
Black bottle
Eetle ottle
Out!

As I went up Hicky-picky hill,
I met two Hicky-picky children.

They asked me this, and they asked me that
And they asked me the colour of my Sunday hat.
Green – G–R–E–E–N spells green,
And O–U–T spells out!

All Join In

. . . and there were present the Picninnies, and the Joblilies and the Garyulies, and the great Panjandrum himself, with the little button at the top; and they all fell to playing catch-as-catch-can till the gunpowder ran out of the heels of their boots.

Samuel Foote, quoted in the Panjandrum Picture Book
by Randolph Caldecott

The games in this chapter range from the rowdy catch-as-catch-can sort to the quietest whispering.

Feet off the Ground
In this form of tag the players are 'home' if they have their

feet off the ground, so people have to get on chairs or stools if you are playing in the house, on steps, low walls, stones and so on if you are playing in the garden.

My Turn

In this tag there are several agreed 'homes' – perhaps a couple of chairs, a stool, a small mat and an upright chair. But only one person may be on each home at one time and as soon as another player says 'My turn' to a person who is already on one of the 'homes' that person must move and can then be chased by 'he'. When 'he' tags another player, that player becomes 'he'.

Blind Man's Buff

One player is blindfolded, turned around three times and let loose to try to catch one of the others. When he does, he must guess who it is by feeling their face and hair – and only if he guesses right does the captured one take his place as Blind Man.

Drum Signals

For this game you need an old saucepan and a wooden spoon – and you also need understanding or far-away neighbours!

One person leaves the room. The others decide on some action they want him to perform, like sitting on a certain chair, standing on his head, crawling under the table. He comes in. One of the other players now guides him by drumming on the pan with the wooden spoon, hard and loud when he is near the right place or looks like doing the right thing, and low and soft when he is moving away from the place or not doing the right thing. When he does what is required, someone else leaves the room and a new drummer is selected. At first the actions must be very simple, but as people gain experience they can get more complicated.

Stations

The players stand in a circle, with one person blindfolded standing in the middle. Each player is given the name of a different station. The blindfolded player calls out, for instance, 'The train is going from Kings Cross to York', at which the two people named must change places while the centre player tries to catch one of them. If he succeeds, he changes places with that player. From time to time, the person in the middle may call out 'All change!', at which everyone must cross the circle to a different place, while the blindfolded one tries to catch one.

General Post

The players sit round the walls of the room with a blindfolded one in the middle. This time each player has the name of a town. The Postmaster General (someone who is not playing, probably a grown-up) has a list of the towns and does the calling out that causes the players to move about, while the player in the middle tries to 'rob the mail' and catch somebody, whom he then changes place with. A game might go like this:

POSTMASTER-GENERAL: A *letter* is going from Scarborough to London. All the children keep very quiet while Pauline and Philip, who are being these towns, *walk* to each other's places.

P-M: A *telegram* is going from Paris to Norwich. Maria and Darren *run* to each other's places.

P-M: A *postcard* is going from Bury St Edmunds to York. James and John must *hop* to change places.

P-M: A *parcel* is going from Oxford to Edinburgh. Michelle and Catherine have to *crawl* to each other's place.

P-M: A *telephone call* is going from Rome to Vienna. This time, Peter and Julie must change places by walking *backwards*.

P-M: General Post!

Tom has not managed to catch anyone up to now, but with everyone walking, hopping, crawling or going backwards, his chances of robbing the mail are pretty good!

What's the Time Mr Wolf?

One player takes the part of Mr Wolf and walks about, while the others follow him, saying from time to time, 'What's the time, Mr Wolf?' So long as he answers by saying it is such and such o'clock, they are safe, but when he replies 'Dinner-time!', everyone must run for home before he can catch them. Anyone caught becomes Mr Wolf for the next turn.

Fish and Chips

Large sheets of paper are pinned up round the walls, each with the name of a shop on it: Mr Sharp the Ironmonger, Mr Rose the Florist, Miss Pinn the Draper, etc., and a list of ten or a dozen articles which that shop sells. The leader who can be a grown-up, calls out, for instance, 'Go and buy me some candles'; the players must find the shop which sells the right article, and queue up in front of it. The last one in the queue drops out (or the last two if it is a large party). Anyone still wandering round after 20 seconds or so, or anyone at the wrong shop, also drops out. The last one left in is the winner.

Rabbits and Ferrets

'Rabbits' hop around with crouched legs and hands on the floor; 'ferrets' lurk in corners and run around on all fours with their stomachs close to the ground. 'Rabbits' have burrows to which they can run home to safety.

The rabbits come out of their burrows and hop around the space in the centre. The ferrets watch from dark corners. At the cry 'Now!' from the umpire, the ferrets dash out and try to catch as many rabbits as they can before the rabbits can escape into their burrows.

The Forester
'He', the Forester, stands in the middle of a circle of 'trees'. Each guest chooses what sort of tree he or she will be. The Forester throws a ball up in the air and calls out the name of a tree. The tree of that name must run forward and catch the ball before it touches the ground, or become the Forester in turn.

Tierce or The Third
This is a game for a large group of at least 10 or more. The players form a circle two deep, that is an inner circle of, say, five with one person standing behind each one of them. One couple is chosen to become Pursuer and Pursued. Pursuer chases Pursued, trying to tag or catch him. The only escape Pursued has is by running into the circle. As soon as he enters the circle he must stand in front of one of the couples. Then he is 'Home' and cannot be caught. But the person at the back of the original couple is now 'Tierce' or The Third. He or she takes the place of Pursued and must run away from Pursuer. If Pursuer succeeds in tagging Pursued, they change round as in most tag games.

Thieves
One player sits on the floor cross-legged with his 'treasure' in front of him. The treasure might be half a dozen assorted objects – a brooch, a couple of necklaces, a bracelet and a pendant. The other players get into position in a circle some way away from him. He is then blindfolded, and armed with a baton made from a rolled-up newspaper. Now the other players try to sneak up and thieve his treasure from him, one item at a time. As soon as one of the thieves

has stolen one item, he must return to the edge of the circle and deposit it. He may then return to the treasure.

The owner of the treasure can, of course, protect his property. If he thinks he hears one of the thieves, he cries out 'Thief, thief!' and strikes out with the baton where he thinks the thief is. If he hits a thief, that thief must return to

the edge of the circle and start again. If he misses, this gives the thieves a better chance to achieve their purpose while his attention is diverted!

Feather in the Air

You need a light feather for this game. The players sit in a circle and have to keep the feather in the air by blowing it. If anyone touches it or lets it drop on the floor, they are out.

Grandmother's Footsteps

'Grandmother' stands alone, facing away from the other players who line up on an agreed line some distance behind her. The players start to creep up on 'Grandmother'. She turns unexpectedly and anyone she sees moving has to go back to the start. The person who reaches and touches her first without being spotted is the winner and may become 'Grandmother' in turn.

Giant Strides

This is similar to Grandmother's Footsteps, with the other players trying to reach 'Grandmother' first and being caught and sent back if 'she' turns round. But Grandmother, with her back turned, also calls out instructions to the players, which they must obey, to do a certain step or steps. A game might go as follows:

Miranda is the Grandmother.

    MIRANDA: Clare, do two pin steps.

Clare must take two tiny steps on tiptoe, hardly moving her feet.

    MIRANDA: Leo, do three umbrella steps.

Leo takes one foot off the ground and whirls himself round and forward, bringing his feet together before he starts on the next umbrella.

    MIRANDA: Jane, do four scissors steps.

Jane, starting with feet together, jumps forward, landing with her feet apart; another jump brings her feet together. This is one scissor step; she does three more.

MIRANDA: Mark, do a two, four shunt step.

Mark has to take two normal sized steps forward, and four back. This step is a good one for Grandmother to use on a player she feels is getting dangerously close.

MIRANDA: James, do a Giant Stride.

And James takes as long a step as he possibly can.

Are You There, Moriarty?

Two people sit on the floor back to back. They hold truncheons made from rolled-up newspapers – and they have stout hats on their heads! When they are settled comfortably they are blindfolded and then the fun begins.

The aim of the game is for each player to try to get the other persons' hat off, by taking it in turns to hit each other with the truncheons.

'I'm not sure I want to play,' said Sophie.

'I do!' said Peter and Darren at the same time.

One player says, 'Are you there, Moriarty?' When the other replies 'Yes', the first one strikes where he thinks the voice came from. It is then the turn of the other to be the striker. And so on until a hat comes off or the players retire to make way for other volunteers.

Turn the Trencher

For this game you need a wooden or metal plate – a round wooden bread board or an enamel picnic plate will do very well.

The players sit in a circle. One person goes into the centre of the circle and spins the platter on the floor. As he does so, he calls out the name of one of the guests, who must leap up and grab the platter before it falls flat. If he succeeds in catching it, he then spins it. But if he fails to catch it he has to pay a 'forfeit'. It's a good idea to have some forfeits thought up in preparation, though later the other guests may invent their own.

Here are some ideas for forfeits:

Stand on your head; do a somersault; eat a bowl of cornflakes with a blindfold on; hop round the circle; creep round the room on your elbows and knees; recite the alphabet backwards; say a nursery rhyme while standing on one leg; walk round the room on tiptoe with a book on your head; get down on all fours like a cat and lap up a small saucer of milk.

The Bank and the River

The players line up behind a string or mark on the floor. The leader calls out either 'On the bank' or 'In the river', and the players must jump to the other side of the line or stay still, whichever is right. If anyone makes a mistake he must drop out. The leader should call out faster and faster.

Card Throwing

For this game you need an old pack of cards and a plastic washing-up bowl.

Put the bowl in the middle of the room and divide the pack of cards into suits between four players. The players stand at equal distances away from the bowl and try to flick the cards into it. The one who gets the most of his or her suit of cards in wins.

If there are more than four competitors, you can organize 'heats', with the winner of each heat playing off in a grand final. Or, of course, you might be able to run to more than one old pack of cards.

Cutting the Ribbon

You will need about three yards of one-inch-wide crepe paper 'ribbon' and a pair of scissors for each pair of players. You can make the ribbon by taking a packet of crepe paper and cutting across it in one-inch widths.

The players are divided into pairs. One holds one end of the ribbon and the scissors and the other holds the other end. At a signal the player with the scissors starts cutting along the ribbon. The first one to reach his or her partner is the winner. Anyone who cuts through the edge of the ribbon in their nervous haste is disqualified.

Balloon Throwing

Each player takes a turn standing on an agreed spot and throwing a balloon as far forward as possible. The spot on which the balloon touches the ground is marked with a piece of card with the player's name on it. The person who manages to throw the balloon furthest is the winner.

BALLOON THROWING

Balloon Bursting
Divide into two teams. Everyone is given a balloon, not
blown up. At the word 'Go' everyone starts blowing up
their balloon. They go on blowing until the balloon bursts.
The first team to burst all their balloons is the winner. The
first ones to burst their balloons can watch other people's
faces both as they blow and as they anticipate the bursting
of the balloon!

Whistle Stop
Contestants are divided into pairs. They stand facing each
other and, at a signal, start whistling. They must whistle
loud enough for the judge to hear and go on whistling until
they have to draw breath. The first to draw breath or stop
drops out. The other is the winner of that 'heat' and goes
into the final or semi-final of the competition. Continue
whistling in pairs against other successful whistlers until a
champion emerges.

Up the Stairs

All the competitors sit at the bottom of the stairs. The
organizer stands in front of them with a coin in her hand.
She holds her hands behind her back then brings them out in
front with the coin clutched in one fist. The players take it
in turn to guess which hand the coin is hidden in. If they
guess right, they move up a step. The first person to reach
the top of the flight wins the coin.

Blindfold Dinner

It is a good idea to have a large sheet on the floor for this
game, and perhaps aprons for the players too! You need
two blindfolds, two bowls of cornflakes and two spoons.
Blindfold two volunteers, turn them around thrice and then
tell them to feed each other. This is another game that
appeals especially to the spectators!

Enjoy Yourself

This is a good way to entertain younger children who may
not be used to being organized into more formal games.
Have a number of things to play with scattered around the
room or around the garden. Divide the players into pairs.
They may choose any game they wish to play and do so
until 'All change!' is called. Then they go onto the next
game of their choice. And so on as long as they wish.

The sort of things you could provide for this are: skipping ropes, a ball, a bat and ball, an Aunt Sally board,
some marbles, some clothes to dress up in, some toy cars, a
hoopla board.

Bun Bobbing

For this game you need a piece of string long enough to be
tied across the room, some short pieces of thin string and
one currant bun for each player. Tie a knot in the end of

the short pieces of string, thread the other end through the
buns and tie the buns to the cross rope. The short hanging
bits of string will need to be different lengths, to suit the

different heights of the players. The buns should be at such
a height that the players can reach them while standing on
tiptoe. At a signal, the players start to eat their buns.
They may not use their hands at all. The winner is the
player who finishes his bun first.

Pass the Rhyme
Players sit in a circle with one person ready to start off the
game with a word. The person on his or her left has to
provide a rhyming word, and then the person on his left
another one, and so on until one person cannot think of a
new rhyme and must drop out. The game can go on until
only one person is left. The words for rhyming should get
more difficult as the game proceeds.
Here is how it might go.
    HARRIET: Mouse.

SOPHIE: House.

PETER: Louse.

JOHN: Douse.

MICHAEL: Grouse.

IMOGEN: Souse.

HARRIET: Oh dear, it's my word and I can't think of one!

SOPHIE: Dress.

PETER: Press.

JOHN: Tress.

MICHAEL: Stress.

IMOGEN: Bless.

SOPHIE: Cress.

PETER: Dress. Oh no, that's what we started with, wasn't it!

JOHN: Television.

MICHAEL: Eurovision.

IMOGEN: Provision.

SOPHIE: Sorry, I can't think of one.

Shop

One person goes out of the room. The others decide what sort of shop they are keeping, and who shall represent the various things they sell. The person comes back into the room and counts to three and then everyone shouts out their own commodity. He has to guess from what he hears what sort of shop it is that he is in. He can repeat the process of counting to three and the others shouting out their wares until he guesses. Someone else then goes out of the room and has a turn at guessing.

Sausage and Mash

The players sit in a circle. One player is given a book and reads from it, but he has to say 'sausage' instead of each word beginning with S and 'mash' for each word beginning with M. When he makes a mistake, the book is passed on to the next player.

Here is a short excerpt from *Tom Sawyer* read for this game:

> In an instant both boys were rolling and tumbling in the dirt, gripped together like cats; and for the sausage of a mash they tugged and tore at each other's hair and clothes, punched and sausage each other's noses, and covered themselves with dust and glory.

To make the game more complicated add further substitute words to the list, like 'tomatoes' and 'apples'. The passage above would then read like this:

> In apples instant both boys were rolling and tomatoes in tomatoes dirt, gripped tomatoes like cats; apples for tomatoes sausage of apples mash tomatoes tomatoes and tomatoes apples each other's hair apples clothes, punched apples sausage each other's noses, apples covered tomatoes with dust apples glory.

How? When? Where? Why?

One player goes out of the room. The others think of a word. The player comes back and has to guess the word by asking people any of these questions.

How do you like it?
When do you like it?
Where do you like it?
Why do you like it?

The game might go like this if the word chosen was 'apple'.

GIDEON: How do you like it?
MORAG: In a pie.
GIDEON: When do you like it?
JESSICA: After lunch.
GIDEON: Where do you like it?

IMOGEN: On a tree.

GIDEON: Why do you like it?

HARRIET: To keep the doctor away.

GIDEON: Oh, it's an apple.

Up Jenkins

This is a very old game in which two teams sit on opposite sides of a table and one team tries to conceal a coin from the other one.

Team A is given a coin and the players pass it between them under the table until the leader of Team B says 'Up Jenkins!' At this point one member in Team A holds on to the coin and they all put their hands, tightly clenched, on the table top.

Team B can now give one of three instructions:

Spider – move hands across the table in a crawling motion.

Beetle on its back – clenched hands are turned over on to knuckles and back again.

Butterflies – hands are placed palm downwards on the table and the fingers are fluttered.

Then Team B guesses who has the coin – if it hasn't actually been dropped by this time! If they guess wrongly they must try again. This can also be played by small groups, of course.

Cat and Mouse

This game has to be played round a reasonably large table – like a dining table. A cat and mouse are selected from the guests and blindfolded. They are then led separately to the table and their hands are placed on it. The cat now has to try to catch the mouse and the mouse has to avoid the cat, but both must keep their hands on the table all the time – until the cat actually makes a grab at the mouse.

The other guests should try to keep quiet so that the two players can listen for the tiniest noise of the other's movements. When the mouse is caught, or after a given time if the mouse is not caught, two other players take over.

Not a Sound

For this game you need a bell with a clapper – like an old school bell. Make an island of furniture in the middle of the room, or draw a circle on the ground. Each person has a turn running round the island, holding the bell in one hand without making it ring. You may *not* hold it by the clapper!

Whispering Hide and Seek
This game is played in pairs. One person from each pair hides. The others are blindfolded. The hidden partner then whispers the name of his or her partner very quietly, and the blindfolded partner has to find the hidden one by following the whispering. You can imagine how confusing this can be with half the players whispering for the others and the rest stumbling around blindfold, trying to find their partner!

Sardines
This is a form of hide-and-seek in reverse, so to speak. One player hides while all the others cover their eyes. Then they all go in search of 'It'. But instead of saying anything, when a player finds 'It' he hides in the hiding place too. Eventually all the players are packed in together in the hiding place as tightly as sardines in a tin. The last one into the 'tin' is 'It' for the next turn.

Blindfold Obstacle Walk
A simple obstacle course is laid out from the door of the room to a finishing point. The obstacles might be a cushion, a pile of books, a bucket, someone lying across the course, or what you will. Volunteers offer to walk this course blindfold. They are allowed to study the course and are then led out of the room and blindfolded. They are brought in one by one and set on the course while everyone else gives advice from the sidelines. 'Watch it!', Mind your step!', 'Lift your right foot!', 'Don't stand on her!'

BUT, while the volunteers are out of the room, all the objects have in fact been removed!

When the volunteer gets to the end of the course, the

blindfold is taken off and the volunteer's face as he or she looks back over the course provides yet another laugh.

Bobbing for Apples

You need some nice rosy eating apples, not too big, and a basin of water. The basin is put onto a plastic sheet on the floor (to protect the surface), and the apples are put into the water, where they will float. Players take turns to kneel beside the bowl and bob for the apples with their teeth. When they get an apple, it is theirs.

Blindfold Candle Snuffer

A candle is stood very firmly on a table and lighted. A volunteer is blindfolded, turned round three times and then has to try to blow out the candle. As you can imagine, this is a sport for the pleasure of the spectators rather than the 'snuffer'.

Munch the marshmallow

Thread a number of marshmallows on equal lengths of thread. Give one to each person. The players hold the ends of the thread in their mouths and then at the word 'Go' draw the thread up into their mouths until they get to the marshmallows and can eat them. The first to finish is the winner.

Farmyard

Guests stand in a circle and the leader says that he is going to go round and whisper the name of a farmyard animal to each person. Then at a signal everyone will make the noise of that animal. However, what he actually whispers to all but one person is 'Don't make any noise at all'. To the 'victim' he whispers 'Make the noise of a donkey'. Then the leader counts to three and, of course, only the 'victim' is left braying like a donkey. You need to be careful who you choose as 'victim' – some one who won't be embarrassed.

Picking up Money

Tell your guests that they can win ten pence if they can pick it up off the floor. Ask for a volunteer. Stand him or her with his back to the wall, with heels touching the skirting board. Then put a ten-pence piece within two feet of his toes. If he can pick it up without moving his heels from the wall and without bending his knees, he can keep it.

When he or she fails, as they will, other volunteers are likely to want to show that *they* can do it.

Word Building

You can use matches or cocktail sticks for this game. The players sit round a table with a pile of matches in the middle. The idea is to spell a word with the matches and not be the last one to finish the word. The first player puts down one match, the next one adds a match to that one as he pleases, so he might make it into an L-shape, he might put in what must be the middle bar of an E or H, he might put a T-bar on it, or he might put the next match along the top at right angles. The next player has to complete this letter; if it is already complete in some form, he may start a new one and therefore decide the word's beginning. Other players go on building up one match at a time until someone is forced into being the last one to finish the word. A word is 'finished' if you can't say how it could be added to.

Here is a plan showing how this game might develop.

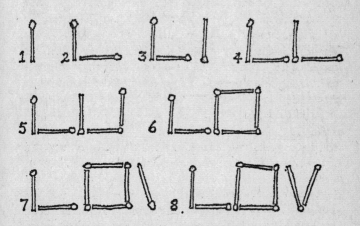

now the 9th move could be
to lead to LOW (lowland, lower, lowest)
or it could be LOVE to lead to LOVE (lovely, lovers)

Passing the Message

This is a good game to play after tea while you are all still sitting at the table, or you can play it sitting in a circle on the floor.

Someone whispers a message to the person on the right of them, who repeats *what he hears* to the person on his right, and so on round the circle. You cannot ask for a message to be whispered twice. When the message has been passed right round, the last player repeats what he or she has heard out loud.

By this time the message has probably become very strange indeed! 'Can I have the cheese?' could well have turned into a 'A can of old fleas'!

Can you Tell Stork from Butter?
For this game each player needs a teaspoon, a blindfold, and paper and pencil. You need to organize in advance, say, ten plates with a different sweet food substance on each – good ones are sugar, raisins, cake decorations, jam, jelly crystals, instant pudding powder, dark brown sugar, icing sugar, cake mixture, marmalade. The plates are lined up on a table. Each player is blindfolded and has to move along the table sampling the various substances and then go and write down the various things that were tasted. The one with the most correct answers is the winner.

Smell It
This game is like the last one, except that it is the sense of smell rather than taste which is being tested. Prepare in

advance about ten narrow-necked little bottles with a different substance in each. Again the players are blindfolded. But this time they have to guess what it is they are smelling.

Likely 'smells' are: vinegar, coffee, washing up liquid, curry powder, garlic, lemon juice, perfume, pepper, orange squash.

And that reminds us of a joke.

A very pedantic scholar was working in his garden putting manure on his plants. His wife was having a ladies' tea party in the house. One of the ladies came into the garden and met the scholar.

'Oh dear!' she said. 'Professor Lipincott, you smell!'

'No, madam,' he replied. 'It is *you* who smell; I stink.'

Feel It

This is another version of the same sort of game. Wrap up a number of items in pieces of cloth and pass them round the circle of players. They have to guess from the feel of the parcel what the object is. Suitable objects for this game are: a light bulb, a hair brush, a slipper, a mug, a torch, a saucepan lid, an egg whisk, an apple, a tennis ball, a pingpong bat.

Easter Bonnets

Each person is given a sheet of newspaper and six pins. With this material they have to make themselves a hat in five minutes flat. They then model the hat, and a prize can be given for the best Easter bonnet.

Match Skyscraper

For this game you need half a box of matches for each player, and one bottle.

The players take it in turns to put one match across the mouth of the bottle, building up the matches more and more precariously. If a match or matches fall off, the player who caused their fall must take them into his supply. The player who gets all his or her matches successfully on to the bottle first is the winner. It is quite in order to place a match in such a position that it is really difficult for the next person not to knock it off.

Pick up Matches
For this game you need a box of spent matches or a box of cocktail sticks. Put them in a paper bag and shake them up. The players sit around the table and one player tips the bag out on the centre of the table. The players take it in turn to pick up as many matches as they can, one at a time, without disturbing the other matches on the table. As soon as they move one other than the one they are trying to get, it is the next person's turn.

You can also play this game only allowing each player to take one match each turn. The player with the most matches when they have all been picked up is the winner.

Don't Spill It

Fill a glass of water nearly to the brim and give each guest a handful of pennies. Place the glass in the middle of a table with the players sitting round the table. Each player in turn slips a penny into the glass without spilling any water. It is surprising how many pennies you will get in if you are careful.

S—PBPG—F

Take Sides

One, two, three, four,
Who do you think we are shouting for?
OUR TEAM, OUR TEAM!
Two, four, six, eight,
The other team's got a tummy ache!

Most of these games are more suitable for parties with ten guests or more, but the earlier ones in this section can work quite well with only six players, three in each team. For a much larger party, the guests can be divided into three or more teams, so that everyone's turn comes round more rapidly.

Blow the Balloon
Each team is given a blown-up balloon. At a signal the balloons are thrown in the air and then have to be kept in the air by blowing only. If anyone touches a balloon to keep it up, he or she must drop out. The winning team is, of course, the one which keeps its balloon in the air longest.

Bean Dropping
In this competition individual members of each team play against each other. Each competing pair is given 10 dried peas or beans and a jam jar per person. They take it in turns to stand upright astride their jam jar and drop the

beans into it. The team which gets the most beans into a jar wins.

You can also play this as an individual competition with pairs playing against each other as a first heat and the winner from each pair going on to play other winners until a champion bean dropper is found.

Stepping Stones

Each player is given two half-sheets of newspaper. Working in their teams, they have to get across a 'river' marked with chalk or string on the floor, always standing on their paper 'stepping stones' which must be moved from behind and placed in front for each move. Only when one team member is across the river can the next member start from the 'shore'. The first team with all its members across is the winner.

Kipper Racing

For this game you need one 'kipper' (cut a foot-long fish shape from tissue paper) and a folded newspaper for each team. The teams divide, half of each team behind a line at one end of the room, half at the other. At the word 'Go' the players try to waft or fan their kipper up to and across the line at the other end of the room with the folded newspaper. Once the kipper is over the line the newspaper is handed to a team member on that side and the fish is fanned back again. The first team in which every member has fanned the kipper over the opposite line is the winner.

Crusts and Crumbs

The players divide into two teams. One team are the Crusts, the other the Crumbs. The Crusts chase and try to catch the Crumbs. Each one who is caught becomes a Crust and joins in the chase until all are caught, when the team divide once more and the Crumbs chase the Crusts in the same way. Lots of exercise, no prizes, nobody has to be 'He' on his own.

Pass the Matchbox

For this contest you need two ordinary matchboxes and two teams. The teams stand in line one behind the other. A matchbox cover is placed on the nose of the people at the front. They turn round and place the matchbox on to the nose of the person behind them, and so on down the

line. You mustn't use your hands to assist you. The last person runs with the matchbox still on his nose up to the umpire. If the matchbox is dropped at any point it must start at the front again.

Pass the Orange

Two teams sit on chairs facing each other. An orange is placed on the ankles of the first member of each team. It must be transferred to the next person, using legs *only*. If it drops it must go back to the beginning again. The first team successfully to get the orange to the end of the line is the winner.

Noughts and Crosses

For this game you need ten players divided into two teams, and nine chairs or stools. The chairs are set out in three rows of three to represent a noughts and crosses frame.

One team is noughts; the other is crosses. They take it in turn to sit in the chairs to try to complete horizontal, vertical or diagonal rows of their members and to try to stop the other team from completing *their* rows. Each player is on his or her own and other team members cannot give advice about where to sit. It helps if one team wears armbands with a cross on them and the other team bands with a nought, in case you can't always remember who you are, who your mates are and who is the opposition!

Bonnet for the Baby

For this game you need two babies' bonnets with ribbons under the chin. If you can't find these you could make two bonnets quite quickly in the 'pixie hood' style by sewing two squares of material together and attaching ribbons at the front edges.

The teams line up behind each other and are each given a bonnet. At the word 'Go' the first person of each team puts the bonnet on his or her head and ties the ribbons in a bow under the chin. Then he turns round and the second person unties the ribbons and puts the bonnet on his own head. In this way the bonnet is passed down the line. The last person to put it on rushes up to the umpire, wearing the bonnet.

Watch out that people really do put it on and tie it properly under their chins. They musn't just throw it on and off their heads!

Get Knotted

For this game you need two balls of strong but not scratchy

string, one for each team. Each team stands in a circle. The end of the team's ball of string is tied round the wrist or hand of one member. At the starting signal, the one holding the string winds it round his body and passes the ball on to the next person, who winds the string round *his* body and passes the ball on again, and so on, until each member of the team has the string round him. Then the last member of the team unwinds the string from his body, winds it back on to the ball and passes the ball on. The first team which has untied itself and got the ball of string re-wound is the winner.

Sweep the Balloon

You need two teams, each armed with a balloon and two brooms. The teams stand behind a line at one end of the room, and a chair is placed at the other end of the room. At the word 'Go' the first player in each team sweeps the team's balloon up the room, round the chair and back to the team, where the next player is waiting with the second broom to take over the balloon. The first team to get its last player back with the balloon is the winner. If by mischance the balloon bursts, another one is provided but it has to be blown up on the spot where the first one burst.

Bag or Balloon Bursting

Teams sit facing each other in two rows. Each person has a paper bag or a balloon on the floor in front of him.

The first person in each team gets up, runs round his team, picks up his bag, blows it up and bursts it (or if you are using balloons, blows it up until it bursts) – unless people have very strong lungs or your balloons are very feeble, the game will take much longer with balloons. As soon as the first bag bursts, the second player gets up,

runs round and then bursts his bag, and so on down the
line until all the bags or balloons are burst.

Ball and Chain
You need balls about the size of tennis balls for this contest.
   Two teams stand facing each other in lines, holding hands.
During the game they must not unlink hands and break the
chain. The two top players, who have one hand free, are
each given a ball. They must pass it down the team from
player to player without the hands being unlinked. If the
ball is dropped, it must be picked up without any hands
being unlinked. The first team to get the ball into the free
hand of the last player wins.

The Girdle Race
For this game you need two circles of strong elastic big
enough, *when they are stretched*, to be passed over the body.
Two teams stand in two rows and at the word 'Go' the
first member of each team steps into their elastic 'girdle',
draws it up his or her legs, over his body and shoulders and
off over his head, and passes it to the next person who does

the same, and so on down the line. The last player pulls the girdle off over his or her head and rushes up to the front of the line with the 'girdle'. The first team with its 'girdle' to the front is the winner.

Dry Whistling Race

For this game you need a cream cracker for each person.

The teams stand in line, each person holding a cracker. At a signal the first person eats their cracker and then whistles loud enough for the judge to hear. The next person then eats his or her cracker and whistles . . . and so on down the line.

Straw and Paper Relay

For this game you need a drinking straw for each person and two pieces of tissue paper. Each person holds a straw and the two pieces of paper are placed on a table.

The teams stand in four groups, half of each team at one end of the room and half at the other. The first person in each team comes to the table with the straw in his mouth, sucks in over the paper so that it sticks to the end of the

straw and runs to a team member at the other end of the room. He then has to pass the paper to the other person's straw, by releasing his sucking as they take over. When the paper is transferred, the second player runs to a player at the other end of the room, and so on until the paper has been transferred between each member of the team. If a player drops the paper, he has to use the straw to pick it up off the floor.

Tiddlywinks Race

Each team is given a large and a small tiddlywink (a five-pence or two-pence piece and a penny could be used instead). At the word 'Go' the first member of each team starts jumping the small tiddlywink with the large, from a line, moving it across to another line about 3–4 feet away. He then picks it up and takes it back to the next member of his team, and so on, until the whole team has had a go. The first team in which all members have taken the tiddlywink over the course is the winner.

Family Coach

The players are divided into two teams, and sit in two circles on the floor. Each player is given the name either of one of the travellers in, or a part of, the Family Coach. In each circle there will be a father, a mother, a coachman, four wheels, at least two horses, a whip, and as many other relations, horses, pieces of luggage and parts of the coach as are needed to make up the numbers.

Then a narrator tells an adventure story which brings in all the different people and things. Every time one of them is mentioned, the player in each circle with that part stands up, turns round once as fast as possible, and sits down. The first one down scores a point for his team. Whenever the narrator says 'Family Coach', everybody gets up, turns round and sits down, and the first *team* with all its members down scores a point. The team with most points at the end of the story wins.

Last Letter Contest
Two teams face each other. The umpire calls out the name of a town or a plant or what you will. The first member of Team A has to give the name of a town beginning with the last letter of the word given. Team B must then provide a town starting with the last letter of Team A's town. And so on down the line until one team cannot provide a name without repeating one already given. This team then loses a life and a new word is given.
A game might start like this:
UMPIRE: London.
CATHERINE: New York.
MARK: Kentucky.
UMPIRE: That's a state in America, not a town, Try again.
MARK: Kingston.
PAULINE: Nuneaton.
JANE: Oh dear! N again! No, I can't think of one.
CATHERINE: What about Nantucket?
UMPIRE: No, too late. Your team have lost a life. Start again. Paris.

Drawing Clumps
Each team has some pieces of paper and a pencil and a table or board to rest the paper on. The umpire has a list of assorted objects like a donkey eating a carrot, a seagull, a daffodil, a cup of tea, a clothes peg and so on. The first member of each team comes up to the umpire, who whispers one of the objects in his or her ear. He then rushes back to his team and draws the object. The other team members try to guess what it is. They may only ask, 'Is it a

... ?' and the artist may only answer 'Yes' or 'No'. When the team guesses correctly, the next member rushes to the umpire, whispers the answer and is given a new object to draw. The team which guesses all the objects on the list first wins.

The game can be made more difficult if the list includes activities rather than objects, like a girl playing croquet, a man mowing the lawn, a dog jumping through a hoop or a cow jumping over the moon.

Or the teams could draw and guess proverbs, like a stitch in time saves nine, a rolling stone gathers no moss, the early bird catches the worm, and so on. Or they could draw and guess nursery rhymes: 'Humpty Dumpty', 'Mary Had a Little Lamb', 'Hickory Dickory Dock', etc.

Knowledge Baseball

Divide into two teams. The leader is the umpire and the pitcher. Mark out a baseball diamond with magazines, like this:

□ 1st

□ 2nd   Pitcher   □ Home

□ 3rd

The pitcher stands in the centre and the first member of
Team A is batsman. The pitcher pitches a question at the
batsman who stands at 'home'. If he answers correctly, he
may run to first base; if he answers wrongly, he is out.
Then the second player comes up to bat. If he answers
correctly, he runs to first base, the first player runs to
second base; if he answers wrongly, he is out and the first
player stays on first base. You continue in this manner
until three players are out and the other team takes over the
batting. Each team scores one point each time a player
manages to get back 'home'. A game might go like this:

PITCHER: What is the capital of Spain?

MARK: Madrid. (He's right so he runs to first base.)

PITCHER: Where is Florence?

PETER: In Italy. (He's right, so he runs to first base and
Mark to second base.)

PITCHER: How many players in a tennis team?

MORAG: Four. (But in fact there are six, so Morag is out
and the other two stay where they are.)

PITCHER: What city is called the Athens of the North?

MICHELLE: Edinburgh. She's right, so she goes to first
base, Peter to second and Mark to third.)

PITCHER: Where is the Monument?

DARREN: In the City of London. (He's right, so he goes
to first base, the others move on with Mark running 'home',

so the team has scored one. The game continues with the second team trying their luck.)

Backward Alphabet
In this game the team with the most players surviving at the end is the winner.

Two teams sit facing each other. Their first task is to supply the letters of the alphabet in reverse order, so if Adam, Sophie and Clare are one team and Imogen, James and Philip are the other team, it would go like this:

ADAM: Z; IMOGEN: Y; SOPHIE: X; JAMES: W; and so on to A. Anyone who gives a wrong letter or hesitates too long is eliminated.

For the next round the remaining players have to repeat the alphabet backwards, but leave out the vowels A, E, I, O, U. Again players are eliminated for a wrong letter or for supplying a vowel. In the final round only every other letter is given, so it might go like this:

ADAM: Z; IMOGEN: X; SOPHIE: V; JAMES: T; CLARE: S.
IMOGEN: No, you're wrong. You're out.
PHILIP: Q.
ADAM: No, *you're* wrong, so *you're* out. R.

As Bright as a Button
This game can be played by individuals, but it is probably better to pool knowledge as a team.

There are a larger number of phrases like the one that gives its name to this game. The teams have to guess the phrases you have in mind from various clues you give them.

You will need cards with a number written on for each phrase, a variety of objects as clues, and pencils and paper for the teams. Scatter the cards about the room and place one clue object on each. The cards should be far enough apart so that one team won't be able to eavesdrop on the consultations of the other!

At a signal the teams have to look at the clues and decide what phrases they represent and write down their answer against the card number on their paper. The team with the most correct solutions within a given time wins. A game might go like this:

Clues	Answers
A button.	As bright as a button.
(Use this as a specimen to explain the game.)	
A feather.	As light as a feather.
A piece of brass.	As bold as brass.
A whistle.	As clean as a whistle.
Two sticks.	As cross as two sticks.
A pin.	As neat as a new pin.
A picture.	As pretty as a picture.
A pingpong bat.	As blind as a bat.
Some soot.	As black as soot.
A piece of silk.	As soft as silk.

Front and Back Race

Two teams sit facing each other. The leader of each team has one empty saucer and one saucer containing an assorted collection of twelve small objects, such as buttons, pebbles, shells and dried beans.

At the word 'Go' the leaders start to pass the objects one at a time down the line. When each object reaches the last person in the line, he or she begins to pass it back along the line, but this time the objects must pass along *behind* the backs of the team.

You can imagine the confusion when people are having to pass some of the objects along the front and some along the back at the same time!

When all twelve objects are back in the previously empty saucer at the front of the line, the leader calls out 'Done!' If all the objects are not back when the umpire checks, then that team is disqualified.

Games Outdoors

Girls and boys come out to play
The moon doth shine as bright as day.

The games in this chapter are best played in a garden or park or on the beach, but most of them are also possible indoors.

French Tag
'He' runs after the other players and tries to 'tag' or touch them on an awkward part of the body, like the ankle or

knee. The person who is tagged becomes 'He', but he must hold on to the place on which he was tagged while he chases the others.

Chain Tag
When 'He' catches his first player, they hold hands and chase the others. Each person who is caught joins the end of the chain. Either end of the chain can tag other players until everyone is caught.

Ball Tag
All the players except 'He' stand in a circle and pass a large ball around from one to another. 'He' runs round the outside of the circle and tries to tag the ball. The one who is holding the ball when it is tagged becomes 'He'.

Target Tag
For this game you need a very soft ball: a baby's cloth one would be most suitable, or even a balloon. 'He' has the ball and tags the others by hitting them with the ball.

Underpass Tag
When 'He' tags another player that player has to freeze where he or she is tagged, arms outspread and feet wide apart. The 'frozen' players can only be released if another player manages to crawl between their legs without being tagged himself. 'He' has beaten the other players if he manages to freeze all of them.

Rhubarb Race
This race is best when there are at least nine or twelve contestants. The players form up on the starting line in groups of three. They stand back-to-back and link arms, so that they look like a bunch of rhubarb tied together. At the

word 'Go' they 'race' towards the winning post, keeping arms linked.

Potato Race
For this you will need an ordinary flat-bladed table knife, two potatoes, and a pan or bowl for each player. The potatoes are placed at one end of the course; the bowls at the other. Each player is given a knife and stands by the pile of potatoes. At 'Go' the players start to transfer two potatoes each from the pile of potatoes to the bowl using only the flat blades of their knives. No fingers; no sticking the knife into the potatoes! If the potato drops, it must be picked up again on the knife. The first one with two potatoes in his or her bowl is the winner.

Bucket Chain
When there is a fire and there is no hose or fire engine to take the water from the water supply to the flames, the quickest way to get it there is by forming a chain of people and passing buckets of water along the chain from the water to the fire. You can practise for such an emergency with this game!

This is definitely a game most suitable for the beach or for the sort of party which is not only outdoors but for which people do not dress up!

You need two buckets of water, two identical jars of about one quart capacity, and two plastic cups.

Two teams sit in rows, with the players one behind the other. In the front of each line is a bucket of water; at the back is the jar. The team leader has the plastic cup. At the word 'Go' the leaders fill their cups with water and pass them back down the line to the last player, who tips the water into the jar. The cup is then passed from hand to hand – not thrown! – back up the line for refilling. The first team with their jar full to the brim is the winner. It is surprising how much water will have to leave the bucket to fill the jar!

Water Carriers

This is really a different version of the idea in Bucket Chain. For this version you need two buckets for each team and a cup or ladle for each. A full bucket of water is placed at one end of the course and an empty one at the other end. The aim is to transfer the water from one bucket to the other, with the team members carrying the water in the cup or ladle in turn. The team which transfers the most water in a given time is the winner.

The game can have added interest if some obstacles have to be overcome on the way from one bucket to another. You could have to climb over a chair or duck under a rope, for instance.

Obstacle Race

This is best played in the garden or park or on the beach. A track is laid out with obstacles which have to be overcome and actions which have to be performed between the starting and the finishing line. You can have obstacles like jumps (a pole laid between two chairs), a large blanket or tarpaulin that you have to climb under, a bench or low wall that you have to walk along, and so on, taking advantage of any natural obstacles on the way. You can have activities to be performed like threading a needle, putting on and racing in some strange garment, carrying a plastic cup of water on your head for part of the distance, filling a bucket of water at a tap and carrying it part of the way, blowing up and bursting a paper bag or a balloon.

This race may best be done in turns against a stop watch, though it can be performed as a relay race between two teams with the runners carrying some object such as a baton, which has to be handed to the next member of the team before he can start on the course.

An obstacle race needs very careful supervision to see that everyone completes every task and to see that all the obstacles are always in their correct positions.

Maze Tag
This is a game for the beach if you are having a seaside party. With a spade mark out a maze in the sand with an area in the middle which is 'home', and some paths which lead to the centre and other paths which have blind ends. The players may only move along the paths and may not jump from one to another. They are safe when they are 'home' in the centre. 'He' tries to tag other players before they reach 'home'. When 'He' tags someone who then becomes 'He' in his place, he may return to the centre to start again.

Longest Long Jump
For this game you need two teams and a lot of space, so it's best played on a large grass space or on the beach (so long as there are not too many other people around who are trying to use the space more peacefully!). Mark a starting

MAZE TAG

line. The first member of each team stands at this line and makes the longest standing jump he can manage. The next person then puts his feet in the exact position on which the first one landed and does his standing jump from there. The third and other players follow on in the same way. The team which has jumped the longest combined distance wins. If you are playing with only two or three people for each team, each person could have two turns to make the longest long jump longer.

Handicap Catch

You need a tennis ball for this game. The players stand in a widely spaced circle and throw the ball from one to another. Anyone who fails to catch the ball is handicapped in one of these ways:

LONGEST LONG JUMP

first drop – must catch with one hand only;
second drop – goes down on one knee, but may catch
           with two hands;
third drop – down on both knees, but may use both
           hands;
fourth drop – down on both knees, one hand only;
fifth drop – out of the game.

But if a player who has dropped the ball catches it on the
next throw, he or she is restored to the previous handicap
position. For instance, if Adam has missed the ball three
times and is kneeling and then catches the ball, he can now
kneel on one knee only.

French Cricket

For this you need a cricket bat and a tennis ball or other
soft ball. The idea of the game is to put the batsman out by
hitting him below the knees with the ball. The batsman
tries to protect himself with the bat. The bowlers (everyone
apart from the batsman) must bowl from wherever the
batsman has managed to hit the ball. Whoever hits the
batsman on the legs takes over as batsman.

Sandpie

This is a game for the beach or for a sandpit. Fill a bucket with damp sand and turn it out to make a sand cake. Put a stone or a birthday cake candle on the top of it. Then each player takes a turn to cut a slice from the cake with a knife or a spatula. The idea is to avoid dislodging the candle or stone from the top and to force someone else into doing it. The first slices can be quite big, but later slices will get smaller and smaller!

Nature Knowledge

This game can be played by knowledgeable individuals, but it is probably better played by pooling knowledge in teams. The host singles out a dozen flowers, trees and shrubs in the garden and ties a numbered label on each of them. The teams then have to identify them and write the name of each plant against the numbers on a list.

Parlez-vous Francais?

This is a version of the previous game which can be played indoors. (if your guests learn French in school). In this game the host ties labels to a dozen household items and the teams have to provide the French words for them. Even *le chien* can be labelled if he will cooperate.

Beach Marbles

Here is another game for a seaside party. It was introduced to us by Italian children on a Mediterranean beach. In Italy you can buy sets of coloured balls about the size of pingpong balls to play it with. But you could use ordinary pingpong balls marked with distinctive colours for each player.

First you need to mark out the course. For this you need the youngest member of the party as a volunteer. He or she

97

sits on the sand, with her hands clasped under her legs and is then dragged round by her feet by the course marker, so that her bottom leaves a furrow in the sand. (You do need very clean, fine sand for this or the volunteer could be hurt.) Then, with a spade or your hands, you mark out a number of obstacles ditches and mounds along the course.

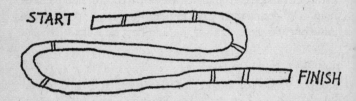

The players stand at the start with one, two or three balls each, depending on how many you can run to. You take turns to flick the balls along the course, with a flick of the thumb against the ball which is held in the palm of the hand. If your ball falls into a ditch, you miss a turn. If your ball goes out of the course, you miss a turn. You can use your ball to knock someone else's ball out of a good position. The first person to get all their balls to the finishing line is the winner. You can then play off for second and third places if you want to.

Trials of Wit

All the games in this chapter require that the players can read, write and/or count.

Kim's Game
Put an assortment of about twenty objects on a tray. Make sure you choose things which are reasonably easily identified and, with younger guests, answer questions about the names of things if they want to know. The sort of things we include on such a tray are:

a pair of nail scissors, a red pencil and a blue pencil, a reel of cotton, a small jug or cup, a felt-tip pen, a small torch, a rubber, a little notebook, a coin, a penknife, a pocket comb, a lipstick, a box of matches, a pepper pot, a teaspoon, a ring, a pingpong ball, a key, a tube of toothpaste, a pocket mirror.

Cover the tray with a cloth. Put it on a table and ask the guests to gather round. They can look at the tray for two to three minutes and then the cloth is replaced and they are given paper and pencil and must write down as many objects as they can remember. Tell them first how many objects there are on the tray. The winner is the one who remembers the most items correctly in a given time.

'But, why,' you may well ask, 'is it called Kim's Game?'

Kim is a story by Rudyard Kipling about the son of an English soldier who wanders around India after his parents

die. At this point in the story he had met Lurgan Sahib, a
jeweller and shopkeeper. Lurgan Sahib has a little Indian
apprentice who is very jealous of Kim, so Lurgan Sahib
encourages the child to show his astonishing skill of observa-
tion and memory to Kim so that the boy can see how much
he can learn from the child.

'Play the Play of the Jewels against him. I will keep
tally.'

The child dried his tears at once, and dashed to the
back of the shop, whence he returned with a copper tray.

'Give me!' he said to Lurgan Sahib. 'Let them come
from thy hand, for he may say that I knew them before.'

'Gently – gently,' the man replied, and from a drawer
under the table dealt a half handful of clattering trifles
into the tray.

'Now,' said the child, waving an old newspaper.
'Look on them as long as thou wilt, stranger. Count and,
if need be, handle. One look is enough for *me*.' He
turned his back proudly.

'But what is the game?'

'When thou hast counted and handled and art sure that thou canst remember them all, I cover them with this paper, and thou must tell over the tally to Lurgan Sahib. *I* will write mine.'

'Oah!' The instinct of competition waked in his breast. He bent over the tray. There were but fifteen stones on it. 'That is easy,' he said after a minute. The child slipped the paper over the winking jewels and scribbled in a native account-book.

'There are under that paper five blue stones – one big, one smaller, and three small,' said Kim, all in haste. 'There are four green stones, and one with a hole in it; there is one yellow stone that I can see through, and one like a pipe-stem. There are two red stones, and – and – I made the count fifteen, but two I have forgotten. No! Give me time. One was of ivory, little and brownish; and – and – give me time . . .'

'One – two –' Lurgan Sahib counted him out up to ten. Kim shook his head.

'Hear my count!' the child burst in, trilling with laughter. 'First, are two flawed sapphires – one of two ruttees and one of four as I should judge. The four-ruttee sapphire is chipped at the edge. There is one Turkestan turquoise, plain with black veins, and there are two inscribed – one with a Name of God in gilt, and the other being cracked across, for it came out of an old ring, I cannot read. We have now all five blue stones. Four flawed emeralds there are, but one is drilled in two places, and one is a little carven—'

'Their weights?' said Lurgan Sahib impassively.

'Three – five – five – and four ruttees as I judge it. There is one piece of old greenish pipe amber, and a cut topaz from Europe. There is one ruby of Burma, of two ruttees, without a flaw, and there is a balas-ruby, flawed, of two ruttees. There is a carved ivory from China representing a rat sucking an egg; and there is last – ah ha! – a ball of crystal as big as a bean set in a gold leaf.'

He clapped his hands at the close.

'He is thy master,' said Lurgan Sahib, smiling.

'Huh! He knew the names of the stones,' said Kim, flushing. 'Try again! With common things such as he and I both know.'

They heaped the tray again with odds and ends gathered from the shop, and even the kitchen, and every time the child won, till Kim marvelled.

'Bind my eyes – let me feel once with my fingers, and even *then* I will leave thee open-eyed behind,' he challenged.

Kim stamped with vexation when the lad made his boast good.

'If it were men – or horses,' he said, 'I could do better. This playing with tweezers and knives and scissors is too little.'

'Learn first – teach later,' said Lurgan Sahib. 'Is he thy master?'

'Truly. But how is it done?'

'By doing it many times over till it is done perfectly – for it is worth doing.'

The Hindu boy, in highest feather, actually patted Kim on the back.

'Do not despair,' he said. 'I myself will teach thee.'

'And I will see that thou art well taught,' said Lurgan Sahib.

How Much? How Many?

You need pencils and paper for everybody and a number of objects displayed on a table with a numbered question next to each object. Without touching the objects, the players have to make a guess at the correct answers. Set a time limit of not more than a minute per object – probably thirty seconds should be enough, so with ten objects allow just over five minutes. An absolutely correct answer scores ten, the nearest correct answer scores five. The highest total score wins.

Here are some ideas for objects and questions.

A tube of Smarties (or box of jelly babies).	How many Smarties in the tube?
A thick book.	How many pages in the book?
A box of matches, half open.	How many matches in the box?
Part of a pack of cards.	How many cards in the pack?
A bundle of string.	How many inches of string are there?
A bit of wood.	How many inches long is this?
A half-empty bag of sugar.	How much sugar in the bag?
A jug of water.	How much water in the jug?
An empty bowl.	How much water will the bowl hold?
A bowl of sugar lumps.	How many lumps in the bowl?

What's in the Picture?

You will need six large pictures from magazines which show scenes with a lot of detail and activity in them. Mount the pictures on sheets of cardboard and hang them up well spaced round the room. Label each picture A, B, C, D, E, F or with more appropriate letters. Give each player a paper and pencil. At the starting signal they have to find as many items as they can beginning with the letter of the picture and note them down. The player who sees the most things is the winner. It is useful to have your own check list, but some people may see extra things besides.

Good pictures for this game would be a busy street

scene, a beach, a shop showing goods on the shelves, the living room or kitchen of a house.

Advertisements

Collect twenty magazine advertisements for well-known products. Remove all the words which would directly identify the product. Number the advertisements from one to twenty and pin them up around the room.

Give each competitor paper and pencil and allow them about fifteen minutes to walk round and write down the names of the products. The one with the most correct answers is the winner.

In another version of this game, Trade Marks, you cut out well-known trade marks, paste them on separate cards and then ask the guests to identify them. As you have to find trade marks which do not actually incorporate the name of the product it's more difficult both to find examples and to identify them.

Sounds Off

Everyone is given a pencil and a piece of paper. A screen is fixed up in a corner of the room or across a door, with a table behind it. The host goes behind the screen and, using various objects concealed there, produces various noises. The players write down what they think the sound is. To avoid confusion it is helpful to call out a number before each sound so that the answers get listed in order on the papers. Here are some suggestions for noises:

Opening and closing a pair of scissors.
Shuffling a pack of cards.
Tearing up a piece of paper.
Clicking your tongue.
Winding an alarm clock.
Brushing a pair of shoes.
Cleaning your teeth.

Clapping hands.
Tapping on the table.
Lighting a match.
Stirring a cup of tea.

Constantinople

Each player has a paper and pencil. A long word, like Constantinople, is chosen and written at the top of the piece of paper. In a given time – ten to fifteen minutes is ample – the competitors have to write down as many words as they can, using the letters in the chosen word. Letters cannot be used in one word twice unless they appear in the original word twice. Real names are not allowed. Some of the words in Constantinople are:

not, cot, pot, stop, pant, pints, polite, constant. The player with the most correct words wins, but players who produce a word which uses letters others than those in the chosen word might lose a point.

This game can also be played with players sitting in a circle and producing words in turn from the chosen word.

Someone who produces a wrong word, repeats a word already given, or can't produce any word at all drops out until only one person, the winner, is left in. It would be helpful to have a blackboard to write down the words already given when playing it this way.

General Knowledge
This game can be quite simple or really difficult to suit the players.

Each player has a piece of paper and a pencil and somewhere to write. They draw a frame on their paper like this:

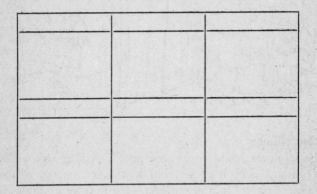

In each heading space they write an agreed subject, like:
town, country, food, animal, flower, plant
girl's name, boy's name, famous person
Then a letter is chosen by the umpire opening a book and, with eyes shut, putting his finger on a letter. (If it turns out to be an awkward one, like J,Q,U,X,Y, or Z, try again.) Everyone has to think of as many towns, plants, names, etc, as they can beginning with this letter and write them into the right place on the frame. The winner is the one who gets the most correct answers in a given time.

Another version of this game is to choose the headings

and then choose a word of about six letters. Divide the paper like this, writing the headings across the top and the word down the side:

	flower	tree	town	country	boy's name	girl's name
G						
A						
M						
E						
S						

In a given time, the players have to supply a word for each column beginning with the letter beside that column. The first column for this example might be:

gardenia or geranium;
amaryllis or aster;
marigold or may;
eglantine or Easter lily;
snowdrop or scilla.

The winner is the one with the most correct answers, of course.

Witnesses

One of the guests, say a girl, is taken out and dressed up in a variety of garments – perhaps a red dress, a blue coat, a yellow scarf, coloured stockings or socks, boots or sandals, gloves, a hat, sunglasses and a shoulder bag. She comes back into the room and walks around among the other guests for a minute or so, speaking to a few of them. Then she leaves the room.

Now all the other guests write down what she was wearing and carrying. They get one mark each for the name of the article and another for the colour of the article. After a given time, the girl comes back into the room and the others check their records with the facts.

Another way to play this game, when you have quite a big party, is for three or four people to make up a scene between them unknown to the others and then to quietly leave the room at some point in the party, dress up if they wish, and burst back into the room and perform their scene and rush out again. Then the other guests are asked what they saw and what happened and what the people were wearing. It helps if some of the questions can be prepared beforehand. It is very interesting to see what sort of things people see when they are 'witnesses' in this way unexpectedly.

Anagrams

To prepare for this game choose a word, write each of the letters on separate pieces of paper and pin them up round the room. The players are given a pencil and piece of paper each and they go round, find all the letters (tell them how many there are first), write them down and then un-jumble them into the chosen word. The first person finished is the winner.

The Möbius Strip

Something to do in a quiet moment.

Beforehand prepare for each person a twisted loop of paper so it looks like this:

Use a strip of paper about a foot long and one and a half inches wide. Fix the strip in a loop with sellotape or glue.

Give each person a pair of scissors and a pencil. Now ask them to draw a line along the centre of the loop without taking their pencil off the paper. If people then unstick their loops, they will find that the line goes straight along *both* sides of the flat strip of paper!

You can now go on to try something else with your loops. Stick them back together. Take the scissors and get ready to cut along the line which they drew on the loop. First ask everybody what they think will happen. The obvious answer is that they will have two separate loops. Try it and see. And then cut it again – and again!

Song and Dance

'*Gaiety. Song-and-Dance. Here we go round the Mulberry Bush.*'
Eeyore in Winnie the Pooh *by A. A. Milne*

Musical Bumps
For this and many other games in this section, you need a
record player and some good jumping around or marching
tunes. Keep the record player out of sight, so players
can't see when it is going to be stopped.

Players dance round the room to the music. When it
stops, they all flop down on the floor. The last one down is
'out'. Go on playing until only an outright winner remains.

Musical Chairs
For this version of the game you need a chair or a cushion
for each player to start with. The chairs are arranged in two
rows back to back down the middle of the room and the
players sit on them. When the music starts they get up and
dance round the chairs and one chair is removed. When the
music stops, they all try to sit down. But of course one person will have nowhere to sit and is out. Go on until only
two players and one chair or cushion are left battling for
who is to be the winner.

Musical Sets
Again the players dance round the room, but in this game

when the music stops the leader calls out a number from one to five and the players have to form themselves into sets or groups of that number. Anyone who is not in a group is out. The leader has to do a bit of mental arithmetic as the game goes along to make sure that someone is out every time. For instance, with a group of ten players, the first call might be 'Four' which would eliminate two players; the next call might be 'Three', eliminating another two. The third call might be 'Five', so that only one goes out.

Musical Objects

For this game you need an assortment of objects like cotton reels, pebbles, pencils and matchboxes on a tray in the middle of the room, one less item than there are players. All the players move round the tray in a circle while the music plays. When the music stops, the players all dive for the tray and grab one object each. The one who fails to grab an object drops out, and one object is removed from the tray. The one who grabs the last object left is the winner.

Musical Hat

The players sit in a circle and, while the music plays, a hat is passed round. Each player must put it on *properly*, then take it off and pass it to the next person. The one who is holding or wearing the hat when the music stops drops out.

Penny in the Tin

The players sit or stand in a circle. Each is given a penny or a small sweet. While the music plays a tin is passed from hand to hand. When the music stops, the one who is holding the tin drops his penny in, and either drops out of the circle, or, if you want the game to last longer, stays in but of course, cannot be 'caught' again. The last player left with a penny wins the tinful.

Pass the Parcel

Wrap a small prize in several layers of paper. Each layer can also be tied with string or ribbon.

The players sit in a circle. While the music is playing, the children pass the parcel from hand to hand round the circle. Make sure it goes quickly and that some people are not holding on to it lingeringly! When the music stops, the person who is holding the parcel takes off one layer of paper or one piece of string. The music begins again and the parcel moves round. The person who unwraps the last layer of paper gets the prize inside.

You can put a wrapped sweet between each layer of paper so there will be more prizes along the way.

In another version of this game, instead of prizes between each layer of paper, there are slips of paper with forfeits to be performed written on them, such as 'do three somersaults', 'balance a glass of water on your head and walk round the circle'. The parcel then, instead of passing lingeringly from hand to hand, speeds round the circle, until a victim is caught by it as the music stops. But put a real prize at last in the middle to make up for the forfeits.

Pass the Hot Potato
This game is the opposite in effect from the last one. There we had to warn you against the person who holds on to the parcel lingeringly; here they may pass it too quickly! You need an object with a smooth surface – a potato, though not a hot one, would do very well.

The players sit in a circle and while the music plays pass the potato from one to another. When the music stops, the one left holding the potato drops out. The game goes on until only one person is left, the winner.

Jumble Sale
Have you ever been to a jumble sale where the customers queue up at the door half an hour before it opens and rush in and grab everything they want to buy as soon as the doors are opened? It's that sort of jumble sale which inspired this game.

An assorted jumble of objects is put on a table at one end of the room, or in the centre of a circle. The players move around to the music, but when it stops they all rush to the table and grab as many objects as they can in ten seconds. The person with the smallest number drops out and a few things are removed for the next round. The game goes on until one object is being competed for by two customers.

Musical Fancy Dress
Put an assorted collection of old trousers, sweaters, shirts, hats, coats and dresses in a pillowcase.

The players sit in a circle and pass the pillowcase around while the music is playing. When the music stops, the person who is holding the pillowcase puts his or her hand into it and takes out the first object touched. She dresses herself in it. The bag passes on with people dressing up from it whenever they are left with it. When the case is empty, there is a fashion parade and the funniest 'model' is the winner.

I Know that Tune
You need a piano and a player with a fund of popular tunes for this game.

The contestants are given paper and pencil. The pianist plays snatches from popular tunes and the contestants have to write down the titles. The one with the highest number of correct guesses is the winner.

Christmas Carols
If your party is in December or is in fact a special Christmas party, end up with carol singing round the piano or, at least, a record of carols played either as people arrive or as they leave.

Traditional Singing Games
Some of the games that follow, or versions of them, may have been played by your grandparents' grandparents when they went to parties as children.

Oranges and Lemons

Two of the tallest children or two grown-ups join hands to make an arch. Everyone else forms a line, holding onto the waist of the child in front, and goes through the arch, singing:

Oranges and lemons
Say the bells of St Clement's.
Bulls'-eyes and targets
Say the bells of St Margaret's.
Brickbats and tiles
Say the bells of St Giles.
Pancakes and fritters
Say the bells of St Peter's.
Two sticks and an apple
Say the bells of Whitechapel.
Old Father Baldpate
Say the slow bells of Aldgate.
Maids in white aprons
Say the bells of St Catherine's.
Pokers and tongs
Say the bells at St John's.
Kettles and pans

Say the bells of St Anne's.
You owe me five farthings
Say the bells of St Martin's.
When will you pay me?
Say the bells of Old Bailey.
When I grow rich
Say the bells of Shoreditch.
Pray, when will that be?
Say the bells at Stepney.
I'm sure I don't know
Says the great bell of Bow.
(These two lines should be sung slowly.)
Then the children begin to run faster as they sing:
Here comes a candle to light you to bed
Here comes a chopper to chop off your head.
The two people forming the arch shout 'Chop, chop, chop, CHOP!', and as they shout the final 'chop' they lower their arms and hold the child who is under the arch at the time. Beforehand the arches have decided which shall be 'Oranges' and which 'Lemons'. In a whisper the child is asked 'Oranges or Lemons?' and, depending on the answer, goes to stand behind one of the arches, holding on by the waist as before. The game continues and when all the players have been captured, and become Oranges or Lemons, there is a great tug-of-war between the two sides – obviously most satisfying if the sides are fairly evenly matched.

Here we Go round the Mulberry Bush
The children hold hands and dance in a ring, first going one way and then the other, while they sing:
Here we go round the mulberry bush,
The mulberry bush, the mulberry bush,
Here we go round the mulberry bush,
On a cold and frosty morning.

Then they stand still and mime, while they sing:

This is the way we clap our hands,
Clap our hands, clap our hands,
This is the way we clap our hands,
On a cold and frosty morning.

Now they dance in a ring again, repeating the first verse. Any number of verses can follow, each alternated with the first:

This is the way we wash our hands, etc.
This is the way we clean our teeth, etc.
This is the way we brush our hair, etc.
This is the way we eat our tea, etc.
This is the way we go to school, etc.

And anything else which may occur to you.

Nuts in May

The children form two lines facing each other, and skip backwards and forwards, holding hands and singing:

Here we come gathering nuts in May,
Nuts in May, nuts in May,
Here we come gathering nuts in May,
On a cold and frosty morning.

Now one side only dances forwards and back, singing:

Who will you have for Nuts in May?
Nuts in May, nuts in May,
Who will you have for nuts in May?
On a cold and frosty morning?

The other side, skipping alone, answers:

We'll have Sophie (or Miranda or Mark, or whoever) for nuts in May, etc.

The first side sings:

Who will you send to fetch her away? etc.

The other side answers:

We'll send Catherine to fetch her away, etc.

Now a handkerchief is laid in the middle of the room, and

the two players named have a tug-of-war, the winner pulls the loser over to his or her side, and the game begins again.

The Farmer in the Dell

The children hold hands to form a ring, except for one who is chosen to be the farmer and stands in the middle.

The children dance round him, singing:

The farmer's in the dell,
The farmer's in the dell,
Hey ho, my dearie oh,
The farmer's in the dell.
The farmer wants a wife,
The farmer wants a wife,
Hey ho, my dearie oh,
The farmer wants a wife.

The farmer chooses one out of the circle to be his wife, and she joins him in the middle. The children sing on:

The wife wants a child, etc.

The wife chooses her child, who enters the ring. The children in the centre may now like to dance too, in the opposite direction to the outer circle:

The child wants a nurse, etc.
The nurse wants a dog, etc.
The dog wants a pat, etc.
We all pat the dog, etc.

And everyone rushes into the ring to pat the dog.

Poor Mary is a-Weeping

The children form a ring, holding hands round one who sits in the middle pretending to cry. The others walk round her singing:

Poor Mary is a-weeping, a-weeping, a-weeping,
Poor Mary is a-weeping, on a bright summer's day.
Oh why are you a-weeping, a-weeping, a-weeping,

Oh why are you a-weeping, on a bright summer's day?
Mary replies:
I'm weeping for my lover, my lover, my lover,
I'm weeping for my lover, on a bright summer's day.
The others answer:
Stand up and choose your lover, etc.
Mary stands up and chooses someone from the circle, who
joins her in the centre, while the others sing:
Now you are married, etc.
And then, standing still, and stretching their hands towards
the couple:
And we wish you joy!
First a girl and then a boy!

Have you Seen the Muffin-Man?
One child is blindfolded and stands in the middle while
the others hold hands and walk round him, singing:
Have you seen the Muffin-Man,
The Muffin-Man, the Muffin-man?
Have you seen the Muffin-Man
Who lives in Drury Lane?
The child in the centre points at random to someone in
the circle, and the nearest one steps forward. The blind-
folded one asks the other three questions, needing short
answers, and then has three guesses who it is. If he guesses
right, they change places.

Act One – Acting Games

The final scene was the grand battle which Lionel had to win against overwhelming odds. I stood waving a handkerchief on a chair, supposed to be a tower, from which I had a good view of the battlefield.

The first to fall was Peppy who, having in the course of the evening been pulled in and out of three tunics to show that she was three separate people, ran on looking extremely tousled, and collapsed thankfully under the bagatelle table. Betty was driven into the audience by Alister. He got her by the foot and she, yelling blue murder and quite forgetting that it was only a play, hung on to the chair on which her father was sitting.

Lionel was chased round and round by Abun waving a cardboard sword, but when all seemed lost Abun remembered that it was his duty to die and so, after giving Lionel one final stab, lay down flat on his back with his eyes shut.

'So perish all traitors,' said Lionel, turning hastily round and putting his foot on the corpse of his enemy. 'Berengaria! My own!'

But at this point the heroine, craning her neck in one last long look for her admirer in the audience, overbalanced and fell off the chair on top of the remaining Dragon who was mauling Peter.

'Oh you fool!' cried the hero.

From Christmas with the Savages *by Mary Clive*

Some people feel very uncomfortable and self-conscious about acting in front of people on their own, but don't mind doing it along with others, when they can feel they are not the only one to be making a fool of themselves! So, if you want to play some acting games, it's probably better to play them when the party has warmed up a bit and to start off with some of the more communal acting games, where individuals don't stand out.

Where Are we Going?

For this game you divide into two teams, each team being the actors and the audience in turn. The actors think of a town and then mime an action for each letter of the name. For example, if the chosen town were Bedford, the mimes

might be: bending; eating; dropping something; flying; opening a door; riding a horse; driving. The audience then try to guess what the town is – they can ask for the mimes to be repeated. Whether they guess or have to give up, it is then their turn to be the actors. Pencils and paper would be a help for the audience in this game.

Please Pass the Salt

The players sit in a circle. One player mimes something he

wants another player to give him. If you are sitting at table and he wants the salt, he might mime the shaking of a salt cellar. If a knitting needle is wanted, the mime would be knitting – it might, of course, produce a ball of wool, instead.

As people get into the game, they will find they can mime more and more obscure objects successfully. All the objects must be readily available in the room – it is no good asking for an elephant or a helicopter!

Me and My Shadow

There are certain 'partnerships' which are familiar to everyone; Miss Muffet and the Spider, Mary and her Lamb, William and Mary, Darby and Joan, Hide and Seek, Bread and Butter, and so on. In this game the players divide into pairs and, having decided in secret what partners they are going to represent, they take it in turns to act their partnership for the rest of the players to guess.

Adverbs or In the Manner of the Word

One person goes out of the room and the others decide on an adverb, for example, crossly, loudly, carelessly, softly, etc. The person outside then returns and asks each player a question – anything he likes, such as What is your name? Where did you go for your holiday last year? What is your favourite food? The questioned one must answer in the manner of the chosen adverb, and having questioned as many as he likes, the person who went out tries to guess what the adverb is.

Alternatively the questions can be put in the following way:

The questioner asks individuals for various actions to be performed 'in the manner of the word'. So, the audience, having chosen say, 'proudly', may be asked to walk, eat, clean teeth, swim, turn a cartwheel, and so on, in that manner. When the questioner manages to guess the word from the way a member of the audience is acting, that person becomes the questioner and goes out of the room.

Dumb Crambo

Working in two groups, actors and audience, the actors go out while the audience chooses a word. The actors, called back, are then told, not the word itself, but that it rhymes with another given word. The actors then take it in turn 'to do the thing they think it is'. You must choose words which have a lot of other words which rhyme with them. This game can be played the other way round, with the actors acting words to rhyme with one they have chosen, and the audience having to guess both the mime, and the word it rhymes with.

Proverbs

Work either in a team or with a partner and mime (no speaking whatsoever!) proverbs for the audience to guess. Here are some suggestions for proverbs that can be shown in mime:

A stitch in time saves nine.
The early bird catches the worm.
All work and no play makes Jack a dull boy.
A rolling stone gathers no moss.
A bird in the hand is worth two in the bush.
Make hay while the sun shines.

Acting Clumps

The players are divided into two teams. A list of objects and/or activities is prepared in advance with objects like:

a seagull, a snail, a hair spray, a teapot, a telephone, a snake, a giraffe, a kangaroo, scissors, a tree;

or activities like:

writing a letter, answering the front door, proposing marriage, fishing, mowing the lawn, watching television.

The groups get as far away from each other as possible, preferably in separate rooms, and the umpire sits an equal distance from each group. One player from each group runs to the umpire who whispers a word from the list to him or her. He then returns to his group and mimes the object or action. The others must guess what it is, with *no further*

help from the actor except a re-enactment of the word. As soon as they guess the word correctly, another player runs to the umpire for a new word. The first team to guess the whole list correctly wins.

There must be no cheating in this game – in particular, the actor must not help his team to guess the word by speaking!

Charades
Teams again, and no team should have more than about five people, so in a large party you may have three or more teams. One group goes out and makes up a play to illustrate a fairy story, song, well-known television serial, book, or

film. They come back and mime to the rest, who must guess what they are meant to represent. If there are more than two teams, then the first one to guess has the next turn. Each group should have a turn, of course. In order to avoid an awkward pause while one group is out of the room, the other group could be deciding on their act, too. If dressing-up clothes are available, so much the better.

Word Charades

The same idea as ordinary charades, but only a *word* is to be guessed, and is acted out in syllables. The actors begin by announcing how many syllables their word has – or, they may say, for instance, that it is three syllables acted as two (it is easier to do 'lady-bird' this way, for example). Then they can either do a mime, or act a spoken scene, in which the 'syllable word' appears. There is a separate scene for each syllable, and finally for the whole word. The others must guess the word.

Syllables can be represented phonetically, so that, for example, in 'perverse', the first syllable could be acted as 'purr'. Some suggested words to use: tremendous (tree-mend-us), address (add-dress), bookmark, sleepwalker, antelope, draughtsman.

Dumb Show

Again you need a group of actors and an audience. The actors leave the room, and the audience decides on an everyday but fairly complicated activity like making a bed, ironing a shirt or doing the washing-up. One of the actors is called back in and told what the activity is. Then a second is called, and the first mimes the activity to him or her. Then the third comes back, and the second actor mimes what he thinks he has seen. Then the fourth actor comes in, and so on. The last actor, having mimed has to say what he thinks the activity is – this is an acting form of 'Pass the Whisper'.

Story in a Paper Bag

This is really a story-telling game, though it could be acted as well. Prepare some paper bags in advance with a number of small objects in them, for example, a toy car, a matchbox, a penny, a feather and a candle. The actors, who can be in pairs or groups, if they would rather, open their bags and after a few moments' preparation, act or tell a story, bringing in the objects in the bag.

Murder Story

The acting is all done by the narrator! The room is made quite dark and the murder story, full of loathsome details, is told as gruesomely as possible. Meanwhile, at suitable intervals, objects are passed round which are said to be various ghastly things.

Examples:

a wet sponge is said to be brains;

a large cabbage, melon or turnip is a head;

a hank of rough wool is hair;

a rubber glove filled with sand is a hand;

cobnut kernels or peanuts are teeth;

a bowl of cooked macaroni is guts;

a dried apple is an ear;

and a small thin carrot is a finger.

This is really a Hallowe'en party game – and it is not suitable for under-tens or the nervous! It might be a good idea for an older person or the party organizer to have prepared a story beforehand.

Treasure Hunting

'When the flag drops,' Antony was watching the starter's hand, 'we can open our envelopes. The list of the things we've got to get is inside.'

Bridget grinned at two people who were staring at her saddleless pony, and took the envelope out of her pocket.

'Go.'

Talisman jumped at the sound of everyone tearing paper.

On the other side of the green Maurice and his partner were reading the list.

'The thing to do first,' he suggested, 'is to think very hard of the best places to get all these things, then make a round of them.'

The crowd on the green was beginning to break up, ponies cantering away in pairs along every road.

'We can get a lot from our house,' said the girl, scanning her typewritten list, 'a letter postmarked in London, a telephone directory, a sweet pea with five blooms, a suitcase.'

'That's fine.'

The green was almost empty now, only a few people with bicycles hung about, some boys were arguing about which was the best way to go first.

'We'll go to a farm for a speckled egg and a pair of blinkers and the hair from a grey pony's tail. We'll have to look out for a geranium in a pot, we may see one in somebody's window.'

'Six 1933 pennies is pretty difficult. Stand, Billy.' The girl's pony was getting impatient now that they were the only riders left on the green.

'A shop's the only place. We'll ask them to look through the till.'

'That only leaves a postcard of Dunkery Beacon, four oak apples, and a picture of a jockey.' The girl tried to conceal her eagerness to start; her odd partner seemed to have forgotten about the hurry altogether.

But Maurice had not forgotten. 'Yes, that's everything except this live caterpillar in a matchbox. Let's go to a shop for pennies first, you know we aren't allowed to split up.'

At a newsagent's, while the girl held Dragonfly and Billy, Maurice bought a postcard of Dunkery Beacon and asked if he could look through the till for 1933 pennies. The woman behind the counter produced a handful of coppers, and he soon collected six of the kind he wanted.

'Two things we can cross off,' said Maurice as he climbed back into his saddle.

'We're doing very well,' said the girl. 'I say, we must win, I've seen the prizes.'

'So've I. And I want one terribly.'

'Quick then, let's dash to a farm for blinkers and a speckled egg.'

Oxus in Summer *by Katharine Hull and Pamela Whitlock*

We have arranged the treasure hunts in this section starting with very easy ones which even toddlers can join in, and leading up to the more difficult ones which can demand quite a lot of brain power and knowledge.

Easter Egg Hunt

This game is obviously meant for an Easter party, but could be adapted for other occasions. You need at least one Easter egg for each guest, but we usually get the little brightly-wrapped ones (more like sweets than Easter eggs) or the white and brown sugar ones which look almost like real eggs, so that we can afford to have more eggs for each person. Hide the eggs round the garden, in fairly obvious places, so that they don't disappear forever and never be found, and at various levels from the ground up to low branches of trees. Everyone is let loose to search, but they are told how many eggs are hidden for each of them. The eggs must be marked with the seeker's initials or each person must be told what colour his particular eggs are. There is usually, in our experience, a final search by everyone for two or three eggs which even the hider can't find, and which are sometimes never found. We like to think that the

birds and mice and other garden animals find them instead.

This game could be played on other occasions with hidden wrapped sweets or balloons, or at a Christmas party with crackers hidden round the house.

Missing Halves

For this you need a number of old Christmas or birthday cards or coloured pictures from magazines stuck on light cardboard. Cut each picture in half and hide one half around the house. Give one of the other halves to each guest and send them in search of their picture. This can be made more difficult by cutting the pictures in thirds or quarters.

I've Found It

Everyone is shown an object which should be small but bright, like a small ball of wool or a toy. Then they all go out of the room. The object is hidden where it can be seen from certain angles. It can be put in a bowl of fruit or among the flowers in a vase, or on a picture frame or lamp.

Everyone comes back into the room and starts searching. As soon as someone sees the object, he quietly sits down. He mustn't touch it or show the others where it is. The last person to discover it is eventually left searching on his own.

Hunt the Matches

Before the party, hide a number of small objects like

matches (or half pennies, though fewer of them) around the room. They can be in quite obvious places, like on a picture frame, among the leaves of a plant, on the crossbar of a table, or on the window sill. At a signal the guests begin to search for them. If it's matches that have been hidden, then the one who finds the most is the winner. If it's half pennies, then everyone has won something. Don't leave this game too late or people will have noticed too many of the hiding places – or even picked up the treasure!

Hunting in Herds
Matches or dried peas or bits of coloured wool are hidden around the room. Players are divided into groups of three or more people and each group is named after a noisy animal – donkeys, cockerels, lions and so on. Group leaders are appointed. The players then search for the hidden objects. But they may not pick one up when they find it. Instead they must bray, crow or roar to call their leader to come and collect it.

Camouflage
For this game you need about twenty small objects in assorted colours. Things like small toys, a ball of wool, a reel of cotton, a button or a teaspoon are good. Hide the objects round the room so that they are camouflaged by their background. For instance, you could pin a blue hand-kerchief to blue curtains, put a reel of green cotton in a leafy plant, a toy car with other things on a shelf and so on. The guests are then given pencils and a list of the objects which they have to find. They then search the room for them, but instead of moving the objects when they find them, they write down on the list where they are. The one who discovers the most objects in a given time is the win-ner.

It Shouldn't Be There!

This game is rather like the last one, except that now instead of being camouflaged the objects are 'hidden' in places where you would not normally expect to find them and it is this inconsistency which is the clue. For instance, you might put a potato in a bowl of fruit, a kitchen knife on the mantelpiece, a cup in the corner of the room, a book in the record rack and so on. The guests are told that they have to find so many objects which are not where they ought to be. Of course, your idea of where things should be and theirs may be different, so if you always keep some things in funny places, they may be 'found' in this game!

Treasure Hunt Clues

You decide a good place to hide the treasure (which can be any small present). Then collect words from newspapers or magazines which direct players to this place. For instance, the hiding place might be 'In the second drawer in the kitchen dresser' or 'Under the bed in Sarah's bedroom', or 'In the right boot under the stairs'. You then have to find the words for the clue and if you cannot find any of the

words complete, piece them together from other words. 'Dresser', for example; might be made up of 'dress' and 'er' from another word, the two pieces of the word being stuck onto a piece of paper. Now hide the words around the room – sellotaped to the woodwork round a window or door, stuck in a picture frame, tucked under a cushion, or pinned to a curtain. The guests are given paper and pencil and they have to go round and find the words (tell them how many there are first). Then they have to arrange them in the proper order to give them the clue sentence. First one to the treasure wins it.

Treasure Hunt with Clues
A really good treasure hunt has to be thought out very carefully beforehand and making it up can give a lot of entertainment in itself. Ideas for a hunt are given below.

The players hunt singly or in pairs. They are given a 'clue' written on a piece of paper. When they work out what the clue means, they can find the next clue and so on until the trail eventually leads to the Treasure. It is best if you can work out separate trails for each pair otherwise it's quite possible for them to follow the pair ahead – in fact, they'd be foolish if they didn't!

Clues can be quite easy, like 'Under Catherine's pillow' or 'Next to the hall table' or 'Look near the dog's dinner'. They can also need a lot of working out. They are often in the form of puns or based on proverbs or quotations. If you're clever you can make up rhyming clues.

Here are some ideas to set you going:
Old Mother Hubbard might have looked in this cupboard
= the kitchen cupboard.
There's no smoke without fire = the fireplace.
Wipe your feet before you do
Enter in and find the clue = the doormat.
Roses are red, violets are blue,

Under a rose bush, you'll find the clue — suitable for a
treasure hunt which also uses the garden.
One, two, three, four,
Listen to us and many more = on the radio.
Hickory, dickory, dock = by the clock.
Have the same number of clues along each pair's trail
and make sure that each trail is approximately as difficult
as the others, otherwise the hunt won't be fair.

A Scavenger Hunt

The competitors in a scavenger hunt can take part in
pairs, in teams or as individuals. Each player or group is
given a list of objects to find or information to collect within
a given time. The list is the same for all players. At the
signal 'Go' they set off on their search. If the game is being
played by teams, the team members can split up to go in
search of different things, but the list will then have to be
longer. The first player or team to collect all the items
correctly and get back to the starting point is the winner. If
no one manages to collect the whole lot, then the winner is
the one with the greatest number.

Here are some ideas for the list. Remember that there
must be enough of each item available for each competing
person or team to collect one, and that the people who
live in the house or know it well have an advantage over
the others and may need to be handicapped in some way.

Objects:

A stone.

A flower.

A bit of string.

A piece of paper.

A paper clip.

A leaf.

A sweet.

A pin.

A book.

A postcard.

A clothes peg.

A nut.

A matchstick.

A paper handker-
chief.

Information:
The name(s) of the family pet or pets.
The number of the house or flat opposite.
The BBC2 programme on at 8 o'clock next Wednesday.
The number of stairs up to the first floor.
The colour of the floor in the bathroom.
The number of windows in the kitchen.
The colour of the roof of the building.
The telephone number of the household.

A much more adventurous version of a scavenger hunt can be played with older guests, who can search the whole neighbourhood for the objects and information, like the children in the quotation at the beginning of this chapter.

Here are some suggestions for this version:
A platform ticket from the station.
The time of the last bus from outside the town hall.
The times of the Sunday programmes at the nearest cinema.
The price of a cup of tea at a certain café (you'd better warn the proprietor!).
The price of a manicure at the nearest hairdresser (not unless it's displayed in the window).
The words on a poster on a certain wall.
A photograph of a member of the competitor's family.
The telephone number of the local library.

One should remember, when compiling the list for a scavenger hunt like this, that one should avoid including things which are going to cause a nuisance to people who are not members of the party – we would think that getting some of the things on Maurice's list in *Oxus in Summer* could have got them into a certain amount of trouble!

All the Fun of the Fair

By two o'clock the transformation was complete. The Four-Storey Mistake had become a fairground, and beautiful it was. The Chinese streamers were gorgeously looped from tree to tree, twined about trellises, and draped over branches. The jovial fish and dragons danced in the light September wind, and coloured masks were strung in unexpected places. The Addisons' tents had been transformed from ordinary olive-drab back-yard affairs to small Bedouin or Arabian shelters. Mona had done this by draping them with anything colourful and handy. A red tablecloth and a green hall rug for one. A yellow bedspread and Father's purple dressing-gown, with the sleeves turned in (and not without a certain amount of resistance from Father) for the other. The result was that the tents were hot as Tophet inside, but wonderful to look at.

Then There Were Five *by Elizabeth Enright*

If you are having a *really* big party and inviting more than thirty children, it is possible to give a Fun Fair party.

At a Fun Fair party, instead of having organized games in which everyone does one thing at one time, there is a choice of side-show games, all going on at once. Ideally, there should be someone in charge of each side-show, so plenty of grown-ups or others who don't want to take part are needed. You should have at least one game to every five or six guests, so that everyone can get a turn pretty quickly.

The side-shows should be set up all round the edge of the room, garden or hall, leaving plenty of room for people to queue up and mill round in the middle – also to run races, of course.

To make it more like a real Fun Fair, you might have a Fortune Teller and A Fabulous Monster.

Fortune Teller
She should have some kind of tent or private place, and be dressed as a Gypsy or Mysterious Oriental, with a veil. You will be able to find a book on fortune telling to give you some ideas on what to say.

A Fabulous Monster
Again, a tent or secluded place the players have to enter is needed. Perhaps a busker outside could call out details of the extraordinary creature to be found within. When the person goes inside, he finds – a mirror! Either a notice, or the person in charge abjures him, 'Breathe not a word of what you have seen!'

Box the Bottle Top

You will need a rectangular table with one narrow end placed against a wall, an empty egg box which held a dozen eggs, and ten or more bottle tops.

The bottom half of the egg box is placed at the end of the table near the wall. The contestants stand at the other end of the table and toss the bottle tops (five for each turn) into the box. The score is two points each for the tops which go into the middle four holes and one point for the tops which go into the eight outer holes (four at either end). Anyone who scores over ten gets a second turn.

Ring Board

You need to take some trouble preparing the board for this game, but as it can be used over and over again it's worth the effort.

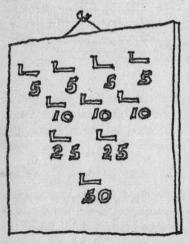

You need a piece of plywood or softboard about eighteen inches square, and ten right-angled screw hooks. Fix the pegs onto the board in this pattern. Paint on the score for each peg. To play you also need five or six small rings – the rubber rings used in bottling fruit are very suitable.

Fix the board on a wall or standing up with supports on a table. Mark a line in front of the board to show where competitors should stand. They throw the rings onto the pegs. The scores are recorded and the highest score of the afternoon wins a prize, or anyone scoring over fifty gets another turn.

Candle Bowling

You need a table in a fairly sheltered corner. Set ten candles on it like a set of skittles – one in the front row, two in the second, three in the third and four in the back row, like this:

Place a pile of books about eighteen inches away from the front candle, on the edge of the table.

The 'bowler' rests his or her chin on the books and can have two blows at the candles in an attempt to blow them all out. Success can bring another turn or a small prize, or champion bowlers can compete for a prize at the end of the afternoon.

Candle Shooting Range

This needs quite a lot of preparation, but the fun makes it worthwhile. You need a dozen or so candles and at least one water pistol. You also need a table with some form of screen around it and a bucket of water. Set up the screen around the table to stop draughts and also to shield passers-by from the 'shots'. Set up the candles in two rows on the table.

A line is marked in front of the table from where competitors must shoot. Each competitor is allowed to fill the pistol three times from the bucket and must try to shoot out all the candles. The winner can be the highest scorer of the afternoon, or anyone who shoots out more than half the candles can have another turn.

Looking Glass Toss
For this game you need a bucket, at least three tennis or pingpong balls, and a hand mirror.

Put the bucket at one end of the course and draw a line for the competitors to stand behind, about five feet away from it. The competitors stand with their backs to the bucket and sight the bucket through the hand mirror which they hold. They then try to toss three balls into the bucket. Anyone who gets in two or more may have another turn.

Magic Square Toss
The magic square in which all lines – horizontal, vertical and diagonal – add up to fifteen has been used as a target board for centuries. Again, it takes time to make the board but as it can be used often it's worth the trouble.

You need a piece of plywood or softboard about eighteen inches square. Divide the board into nine equal squares and paint the dividing lines on the board. Paint the numbers of the squares in, like this:

Lay the board on a table or on the ground.

2	9	4
7	5	3
6	1	8

The competitors stand at an agreed distance from the board and toss two pence pieces or draughts onto the board. You can only score with the pieces which land inside a square, not touching or crossing the lines. The person who scores fifteen is the winner – if anyone does!

Cover the Coin
You need a plastic washing-up basin full of water, a coin (fifty pence or ten pence, depending on how rich you feel!) and a number of two pence pieces or metal discs about that size. Competitors try to cover the coin in the bowl by dropping their coins or discs onto it from an agreed height, kneeling on a chair perhaps. The person who covers the coin wins it.

This is much more difficult than it sounds because the water deflects the dropping coin.

Squails
This is a very ancient game. For a 'squail' a draught will do, although originally it was a doughnut-shaped object. You can mark out a squail board on a card table or ordinary kitchen table. Draw a large chalk circle on the table so that its circumference comes to about four or five inches from the edge of the table. Mark a spot in the middle of the circle.

Each player has four draughts. The aim is to snap the draughts or squails from the table edge towards the centre spot, using the middle finger against the thumb. The winner is the one whose squail ends up nearest to the centre spot.

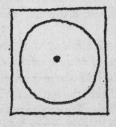 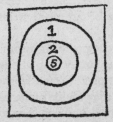

You can add further circles to the board, like a target, and give a score for each circle. And you can make the game more competitive if you knock your opponents' squails out of positions of advantage with your own.

Jets
All the players are given a different coloured balloon. They stand behind a line and blow up their balloons as far as they can, holding onto the mouth of the balloon to stop the air escaping. At the word 'Go' they release the balloons so that they jet forward on the escaping air. The balloon that travels furthest – in the right direction! – is the winner.

Pin the Tail on the Donkey
For this competition you need a blackboard or a large piece of paper which you can pin on the wall, some lengths of thick string, and drawing pins.

Draw the outline of a donkey on the blackboard or paper. Make 'tails' out of the string with a drawing pin fixed at one end.

Each competitor in turn is blindfolded and has to walk up to the donkey from about six feet away and pin a tail in the right place. You'll be surprised where it goes!

Mark the position of the tail with the initials of the person who pinned it there. The winner is the person who pins their tail nearest to the target.

Walk Straight

Lay a piece of string or tape straight down the room or across part of the lawn. The players are given a pair of binoculars or opera glasses and must walk along the tape looking at their feet through the *wrong* end of the glasses. Try it yourself to see what happens!

Races

During the afternoon you could have a series of races – using all the old traditional ones like a three-legged race (competitors stand together in pairs and the right leg of one and the left leg of the other are tied together, so they have to run with 'three legs'); a sack race (each competitor gets into a sack and has to hop and run as best he can to the finishing post); a wheelbarrow race (another partnership race, in which one competitor goes down on his hands and the other one picks up his legs and trundles the 'wheelbarrow' down the course); an egg and spoon race (each competitor is given a spoon and an egg – preferably hard boiled! – and has to run down to the finishing line without dropping the egg); a somersault race (competitors reach the finishing line with a series of somersaults); a skipping race if you have enough skipping ropes or suitable lengths of rope to go round; a leap frog race (pairs working together, the first person bending down hands on knees, partner leaps over and bends down himself – with an agreed number of frogs and leaps to the end of the course to stop any argument about people running too far between leaps!)

Aunt Sally

You need to prepare an Aunt Sally board for this game and also some bean bags. The board could be made from stiff cardboard. Paint the face of a fat lady with a big, smiling, gaping mouth on the cardboard. Cut out the mouth.

You can also cut round the face if you like. This is Aunt Sally. You will need to make at least three bean bags. Cut two four-inch squares of cloth for each bag. Sew the two pieces together along three sides. Turn the bag you have made inside out. Half fill with dried peas or beans (half a pound should be plenty for three bags). Sew up the fourth side.

Stand the Aunt Sally against a wall. Competitors stand at an agreed distance away and try to throw the bean bags into Aunt Sally's mouth. Try it yourself first to make sure that her mouth is big enough.

You could use pingpong balls as missiles if you haven't the time to make bean bags.

Treasure Island

Draw a map of the Treasure Island as large as you conveniently can. It should show rivers, forests and hills, as well as pirates, skulls and crossbones and so on, if you can manage it; think up sinister names for the places such as Dead Man's Gulch and Skeleton Wood.

This map is pinned to a board, after a small cross has

been secretly marked on the back of the map by someone who will not be playing. There should be a pin attached to a small paper flag with his or her name on for each guest. The one whose pin is nearest the secret cross wins the treasure.

A bag of gold and silver chocolate coins makes a good treasure.

A Bran Tub

If you want to give your guests a small present as they go home, a Bran Tub is an appropriate way to do it at a Fun Fair party; it can be used at other parties too, of course.

Either each present has its owner's name on it, and is pushed back into the bran if found by someone else, or all the presents are the same, or all the girls' and all the boys' presents are the same and wrapped in two different coloured papers.

Farewell

When tea was over the children went back to the hall and put on their hats and coats, and as they went out a smart footman at the door gave each child an orange, an apple, and a bag of sweets.
Ameliaranne and the Green Umbrella *by Constance Heward*

There are two rather awkward moments at a party – at the beginning when everyone is arriving, and at the end when everyone is going. Both are times when it helps a great deal to have more than one grown-up on hand – one to be greeting the guests and taking their coats, or greeting the parents and finding the coats, and one to be organizing the games. Both are times when the games have to be such that you can drop into or out of them without spoiling them for everybody else. If, for instance, a game 'where you can win prizes' is being played, nobody will want to be dragged away from it! Also, a team game will be spoiled if one or two members have to go. Games like 'Musical Statues' (in which everybody dances round to music and when it stops 'freezes', and someone judges which is the strangest attitude), Hide and Seek and most Tags are all right. There is also 'Tommy', which is Sophie and Miranda's game:

Tommy
All the guests sit in a circle. In the centre a napkin is laid down, with five sweets tastefully disposed upon it. It is very

important that the sweets should all be different, and of different degrees of desirability. In turn, one person is sent out of the room, and the others choose one sweet to be Tommy. Then the one outside is called back and can take and *keep* any sweet that is *not* Tommy. If he is unlucky enough to pick Tommy first, then he gets no sweets, but if Tommy is left to the last, then he is allowed to have him, too.

This is gambling combined with some psychology – if your friends know you like lollipops, would they expect you to think that they have chosen one? – while they have actually chosen a wine gum, which they know you like least.

It is usual (but not compulsory) for each guest to be given a parting present as they go. This should be something quite small. For the very young, a couple of balloons will give as much pleasure as anything; for older children you might give a colouring-book, a box of coloured chalks, a small model car, a Woolworth's ring, a bubble-blowing outfit, a 'long tongue' paper whistle, a small magnet, or a tiny article of doll's house furniture. One used to be able to get lots of little things for sixpence or a shilling, which is about right, but now you may find it hard to find things which cost less than ten or fifteen pence.

You can just give the guests their presents as they go or you can make more of an occasion of it. At a Christmas party, Santa Claus can arrive or the presents can hang on the tree; at Easter you can hide tiny Easter eggs and have a hunt for them (page 128), you can have a bran tub (page 145) or you could have an:

End of the Rainbow Treasure Hunt
Each child is given a piece of wool (you use as many different colours as there are people). Everyone must search for his own present, which will be tied up with the same coloured wool as the 'clue'. If you play this as the going-home game, you can make the hiding places quite difficult

and all over the house. You may have to help a guest whose parents want to go — for this reason as well as others, it's a good idea to have a list of where each person's present is hidden.

Thank You and Goodbye

'And remember, my dear children, to behave civilly and politely to everybody.'

History of the Fairchild Family *by Mrs Sherwood*
First published *1818*

This chapter is not for the people who have given the party, but for their guests.

Many children just grab all their prizes and presents and hurry away when their parents call for them at the party's end, without a word of thanks or goodbye.

To find your host or hostess and say 'Goodbye and thank you for having me – it was a lovely party' or 'I have enjoyed

myself', is no trouble to the guest but means a great deal
to the person or people who arranged the party and worked
so hard to give you a good time.

If you have enjoyed this PICCOLO Book you may like to choose your next book from the titles listed on the following pages.

Piccolo Puzzles and Games

Piccolo Funny Books

Margaret Gossett
PICCOLO BOOK OF JOKES (illus) 20p

Farmer: What do you use to treat a pig with a sore throat ?
Vet: Oinkment.

The best way to treat yourself – to a good laugh! – is with this hilarious collection of Jokes, Howlers, Limericks, Puns and Shaggy Dog stories. But be warned! Piccolo Books can't be held responsible for the consequences if you laugh out loud while reading this book in public!

edited by Biddy & Rosemary Gill
**THE BLUE PETER BOOK OF
   LIMERICKS** (illus) 20p

'An award-winning programme Blue Peter,
Asked for limericks with plenty of metre,
  They arrived host by host,
  Inundating the post,
And buried poor Val, John and Peter!'

– and that's what nearly did happen! So many of the 8,000-plus entries received by Val, John and Peter were really good that it was possible to put the best into a book – and here they are, together with a special introduction by your Blue Peter favourites which tells you about Limericks and their history.

More Piccolo Puzzles and Games

David Webster
BRAIN BOOSTERS (illus)   20p

Here are 300 Science Riddles, Puzzles and
Brainteasers – an intriguing voyage of dis-
covery for the curious of all ages! Meet the
Bleeps and the Fubbyloofers ... learn how
to make balloon-rockets and identify finger-
prints. ... experiment with thermometers
and wham-wham jars ... Each section has
something for everyone – entertaining, infor-
mative and definitely Brain Boosting!

John Jaworski and Ian Stewart
NUT-CRACKERS (illus)   20p

Puzzles and games to boggle the mind! You'll
find all sorts of things to do, things to make
and things to look at in this entertaining book
– word games, code games, string puzzles,
mazes, number patterns, skeleton crosswords
– and not forgetting of course Professor Crank-
shaft's Impossible Objects!